PRAISE FOR PURPOSE WILL PREVAIL

"Our purpose is a gift from God. It is an opportunity for us to reciprocate God's love for us in service to others. You don't have to search outside of yourself to discover your purpose. You were created and born with a divine purpose within. Jasma Starks beautifully and clearly illustrates how the power of activating and walking in your purpose provides you with the peace and personal power to prosper in your life. *Purpose Will Prevail* is a must read for anyone who desires to be all they were created to be, please God, and live a purpose-full life."

--**Catrice M. Jackson,**

International Best-Selling Author and BOSSLady of Branding | www.bossladyofbranding.com

"Purpose will Prevail takes a look at life through a lens of powerful truths. It takes you along an insightful journey of discovering keys to live the way you were designed to. Its pages explain why so many feel unfulfilled and how purpose will always prevail. By using a refreshing combination of inspirational concepts, personal testimony, and practical wisdom, Jasma Starks writes a message that everyone must understand."

--**Duaine Johnson,**

Pastor of Purpose Church and Founder of MFB Global

"Purpose will Prevail: Principles to Activate and Walk in Your Divine Purpose is a timely book that speaks to each one of us who are breathing. Jasma Starks has given us the keys to open our destiny and go after why we were created!"

--Joshua Jackson, PharmD.

"As I'm reading *Purpose will Prevail,* I receive news that a 15-year-old girl has committed suicide. If only she would have known she had been created with a purpose. I believe Jasma Starks has heard from God and this book is a "now word" for many who need to know their Creator and that He has created them with a specific purpose."

--Glenda Ellison

PURPOSE WILL Prevail

Principles to Activate and Walk in Your Divine Purpose

JASMA STARKS

PURPOSE WILL PREVAIL
Copyright © 2015 Jasma Starks

All rights reserved. No part of this book may be reproduced, distributed or transmitted in any form by any means, graphics, electronics, or mechanical, including photocopy, recording, taping, or by any information storage or retrieval system, without permission in writing from the publisher, except in the case of reprints in the context of reviews, quotes, or references.

Scriptures marked NIV are taken from the Holy Bible, *New International Version*®, NIV®. Copyright © 1973, 1978, 1984, 2011 by Biblica, Inc.™ All rights reserved.

Scriptures marked NKJV are taken from the Holy Bible, New King James Version®, NKJV®. Copyright © 1982 by Thomas Nelson. All rights reserved.

Scriptures marked NLT are taken from the THE MESSAGE. Copyright © 993, 1994, 1995, 1996, 2000, 2001, 2002 by Eugene H. Peterson. All rights reserved.

Scriptures marked MSG are taken from the Holy Bible, New Living Translation. Copyright © 1996, 2004, 2007, 2013 by Tyndale House Foundation. All rights reserved.

Published by: Purposely Created Publishing Group™

Printed in the United States of America

ISBN-10: 1-942838-09-3
ISBN-13: 978-1-942838-09-8

Special discounts are available on bulk quantity purchases by book clubs, associations and special interest groups. For details email:
Sales@PublishYourGift.com or call (866) 674-3340.

For more information, log onto
www.PublishYourGift.com

DEDICATION

I dedicate this to my Lord and Savior Jesus Christ for the opportunity He has entrusted me with to be able to spread the Good News. I am beyond grateful for what my heavenly father is doing in my life. Through everything, the darkest moment, and the moment of unspeakable joy, you have been there. You have never left me nor forsaken me. Many times I have tried to go my own way, but you have kept me through it all. Your grace and mercy is forever faithful. Jesus, I love you!

To my wonderful husband, Ravon Starks Sr., thank you for walking with me on this journey and the long nights of reading page after page. Thank you for your forgiveness that keeps us fresh and in love. To my children, Jeremiah, Jayden, and Ravon Jr., thank you for pushing me to a better place in Jesus Christ. Your prayers empower me to push forward and to walk in all that God has for me.

To my mother and father, Jesse Jackson Sr. and Lee Ellen Sykes, thank you for supporting me no matter what. God ordained you both to be my parents, and I am so glad about it. I honor you both and love you beyond the grave.

To my brothers and sister, Jesse Jackson Jr., Joshua Jackson, Jason Jackson, Jeremy Jackson, Justin Sykes, and Mary Jackson, thank you for everything—the good and the bad. We have grown nothing but stronger together. I love you all with everything in me.

I dedicate this book to you!
Walk in your purpose, and let nothing stop you!

CONTENTS

Dedication		iii
Foreword		ix
Introduction		xiii
1	Designed with Purpose	1
2	Purpose Interrupted	13
3	Purpose Activated	27
4	The Process of Purpose	39
5	The Unexpected: My Testimony	57
6	Deliverance: Breaking the Power of Addiction	73
7	Breaking the Spirit of Fear	81
8	Protecting Your Purpose	97
9	Trusting God with Your Purpose	111
10	A Divine Release into Purpose	121
Bibliography		131
About the Author		133

FOREWORD

BY DR. KOOKIE SCOTT

What an awesome realization to wake up one day and find out that your stay here on earth is far more gratifying than the consumption of oxygen, space, and time. It is an amazing blessing to find out that you were called and given a PURPOSE to actually be here. I have been a born again Christian since 1969, and it has been a journey.

When one takes on the spiritual likeness of a Godhead, there is a requirement to walk, be, and relate within the likeness of the deity. This synergistic relationship will reveal your own identity, oneness and sense of PURPOSE, as well. Every single day of walking in Christ has been like picking fruit from a tree.

To follow the harvesting analogy of picking fruit, apples are delicious to eat. However, some are sour and may house a resident, a hidden worm crawling throughout its core. As you're reaching to get that apple, you may cause three or four more to ping you on the head. But through it all, if you don't give up on your objective, you'll find a few sweet ones that will nourish you. As the saying goes, "An apple a day keeps the doctor away."

I've known Jasma for many years and it is an honor to know from whence she has come, to this awesome time in her life. Being her pastor for 12 years (the number of discipleships) has been a journey. Part of the intrigue and reality of ministry is the constant reminder, realization and application of the concept that no two people on earth have the exact same mission, job or PURPOSE. Each of us is here to do, provide, facilitate, and/or address a certain job; in that way, our callings are fulfilled.

The world is here, and we are here to share it. Let's get to work and find what our purpose is. As pastor to Jasma, it is awe inspiring to observe as she moves into her place of destiny and further effectuates her share of this big world. She has come full circle in her abilities and desires to express many points of our study, focus and meditations that were taught in our congregation. As I recall, Jasma was quietly attentive as she deeply absorbed our topics of discussion while in Bible Study. And we're at the flash point of her knowledge and wisdom as she moves forward to further challenge us on PURPOSE.

It brings a smile to my heart to know that as you read this book, you'll be able to picture this young girl who gave her life to God as a tender teen, who truly sought the Lord as the Holy Spirit made His residency in her life. I've encountered many things in my own life, but the one thing that pushed my reluctant heart aside and pressed it toward the higher calling in Christ Jesus was my realization that I, too, had PURPOSE.

What a wonderful thing to know that all you have encountered in your life was fashioned only to push someone else to his or her destiny. Hopefully, you have, or will, realize that arriving at your destiny will take perseverance and an old fashioned *I ain't gonna quit* in your spirit. I am so grateful that my PURPOSE allowed me to be in Jasma's life. I believe that a person will live longer once they realize they have a purpose to complete a God given charge and a task rather than just meandering through life, not knowing what they are to do. PURPOSE gives you a reason to wake up and go to sleep, to forgive, and mostly to live. Enjoying this book will fulfill the empty part of you that asks such things as why me, what's this for, and how long do I walk in this. Take this journey and understand that God created YOU for PURPOSE with PURPOSE, GIVING you PURPOSE TO fulfill the work set before YOU.

--Dr. Kookie Scott

INTRODUCTION

Purpose is a misconceived subject when it comes to mankind. Purpose is so much greater than what we are taught throughout our life. We are taught that purpose is what you want to be when you grow up, how much money you can make on a job, or maintaining a certain career status. Purpose is so much more than what we can see with our natural eyes; it's something we were created with. We don't have to go to school to get it because it is the very inner part of our being. A life without purpose is a life unfulfilled, having no power or authority. Only when you know who you are do you possess a power that will cause your presence to produce authority.

Often times we do not have a clue of what purpose really is, or how to figure out what it is. This book will take you to another level in your faith and your purpose. You will grasp the understanding that purpose is greater than thy self. I will take you on a journey through this book to unlock, activate, and release your purpose into the earth. Jesus had a wonderful mission that only he could fulfill; nobody could have walked in his shoes if they tried. No one could copy what he was created to do, and the same is for you. No one can walk in your shoes, and no one can fulfill your purpose but you.

Purpose Will Prevail

This world is full of distractions and keeps us from fulfilling our God-given purpose. Although purpose continues to be interrupted through life and unexpected circumstances, there is hope for those who are lost. Hope that fills every void when we are confused and afraid of what is to come. While reading this book, your purpose will be activated inside of you. You will no longer sit in a stagnant place in your life, but you will want to do what you are called to do. Activation takes participation on our part. We have to do the work. If we do our part, God will do His. Life is a process and so is purpose. We become uncomfortable and dissatisfied with the process of purpose and lose heart for what we are called to do. I will show you a way to embrace the process in a way that will captivate your mind and change your outlook on pressure.

I uncover some dark moments in my life that tried to keep me from my purpose, but by the Spirit of God, I was able to overcome every distraction and trap that was set for me to stumble and fall. No matter the circumstance or situation, you have to fulfill your purpose. That is what you were created to do. There are many things and misconceptions that gravitate to us—that tell us we cannot do what God has called us to do. Well, that breaks today. You are well-equipped and capable of living a purpose-filled life.

We tolerate the wrong things, and fear is what keeps us in that place. I walk you through steps of breaking the spirit of fear and addictions. These two things are the most powerful in keeping us captive. Protecting your purpose is highly important and I give you principles to carry it and successfully birth it into the world. We have to trust God with what He has placed in us for this journey. You will not be disappointed. For what God has planned for you is greater than you could ever think or imagine.

Purpose will Prevail sets a standard for people to understand that they were created with a purpose that only they will fulfill in covenant with God. Sin causes separation from God and plays a huge role in us not fulfilling our purpose.

Through striking stories, applicable analogies, and tangible testimonies, *Purpose will Prevail* creates an appetite that takes a person from a place of stagnancy to one of divine release. If we use the power inside us to break strongholds and stand, God will gracefully use His to release us into purpose.

Jasma

1

Designed with a Purpose

How blessed is God! And what a blessing he is!
He's the Father of our Master, Jesus Christ,
and takes us to the high places of blessing in him.
Long before he laid down earth's foundations,
he had us in mind, had settled on us as the focus
of his love, to be made whole and holy by his love.

(Ephesians 1:4, The Message)

There is one person responsible for your purpose and why you were created. If it gets fulfilled or not is totally up to you. God chose you before the foundation of the world—yes, *you*! It amazes me that God had a plan and a purpose for you before you entered your mother's womb. Let's take a second to expound on this: There are about 7 billion people in the world today, and God chose you. I want you to get this in your soul and spirit. You were chosen for greatness beyond human comprehension. Once I came to the realization of how important it is to know who God is, who I am, and why I'm here, my mindset completely changed about how I viewed myself and my life. See your life how it was created to be, not by your surface-level thinking.

Purpose Will Prevail

> *Oh yes, you shaped me first inside, then out;*
> *you formed me in my mother's womb.*
> *I thank you, High God—you're breathtaking!*
> *Body and soul, I am marvelously made! I worship*
> *in adoration—what a creation! You know me inside*
> *and out, you know every bone in my body;*
> *You know exactly how I was made, bit by bit,*
> *how I was sculpted from nothing into something.*
> *Like an open book, you watched me grow from conception*
> *to birth; all the stages of my life were spread out before*
> *you, The days of my life all prepared before I'd even lived*
> *one day* (Psalms 139:14, The Message)

This scripture blows my mind. God created each and every one of us uniquely. Not one of us are the same. We are fearfully and wonderfully made. If God created us before the foundation of the world, that means He put everything in us that we need to fulfill our purpose that was designed for us here on earth. God's intentions for us are good, and He has a plan for us to prosper in all that we do. *For I know the plans I have for you, "declares the* LORD, *plans to prosper you and not to harm you, plans to give you hope and a future" (Jeremiah 29:11, NIV).* Jeremiah 29:11 tells me that God has great plans for me; plans that will not harm me while I am going through the process to fulfill my purpose. We have to go to Him, however, to find out what that purpose is. Oftentimes, we look to the wrong source to give us guidance and information about our calling when the one who created us has all the answers. God majors in purpose, He *is* purpose, and whatever He does and speaks is on purpose.

Let's go to the beginning where it all took place, where God created man in His own image. We are all created in the image of God. When God created us, He put some of Him in us. Do you understand how powerful that is? The creator of the universe said I want to make man look like me. I want you to put your name in place of man. Say it with me, "I want to make (insert your name) look like me." Wow, to imagine the righteousness and holiness of God is beyond my human comprehension. Let's take a look at Genesis 1 and 2:

God spoke: "Let us make human beings in our image, make them reflecting our nature. So they can be responsible for the fish in the sea, the birds in the air, the cattle, And, yes, Earth itself, and every animal that moves on the face of Earth." God created human beings; he created them godlike, Reflecting God's nature. He created them male and female. God blessed them: "Prosper! Reproduce! Fill Earth! Take charge! Be responsible for fish in the sea and birds in the air, for every living thing that moves on the face of Earth (Genesis 1:26-28, The Message)."

At the time GOD made Earth and Heaven, before any grasses or shrubs had sprouted from the ground—GOD hadn't yet sent rain on Earth, nor was there anyone around to work the ground (the whole Earth was watered by underground springs)—GOD formed Man out of dirt from the ground and blew into his nostrils the breath of life. The Man came alive—a living soul! (Genesis 2:5-7, The Message)

Purpose Will Prevail

In Genesis 1, God made man in His image. God created human beings godlike, mirroring His nature and image. He created us both male and female; this is where He created YOU. He blessed you and gave you authority. Authority is one of the main attributes needed to fulfill your God-given purpose.

Now look at Genesis 2. God had made heaven and earth, but there was no grass or plants growing from the ground. God hadn't sent rain on the earth, nor was there anyone around to work the ground. So God formed man, and He did so out of dirt from the ground and blew into his nostrils the breath of life. The man came alive. Do you see what I see? God didn't physically make man until Genesis 2. Before you were conceived in your mother's womb, you were with God, waiting to be sent into the world at an appointed time. The appointed time is the year you were born. Don't take lightly the year you were born and the reason you were sent to the earth. There are people who will be radically changed and things that need to be done because of your very being.

Now that you know that you were created before the foundation of the world, let's look at some biblical examples. The three people I will speak of are Jesus, Samson and Moses. These three people changed the face of the earth. Each one of these stories are different, showing how intentional God is in creating people for specific purposes.

Jesus: Before Jesus came into the world, God had a plan and purpose for his life. God knew the end since the beginning. How do we know Jesus was designed before the foundation of the world? Prophecy! There were many prophecies spoken of the birth of Jesus and how he would transform the world. Prophecy is a statement of what will be before it happens. *Therefore the Lord Himself will give you a sign: Behold, the virgin shall conceive and bear a Son, and shall call His name Immanuel (Isaiah 7:14, NIV).* Here's a word you can take to heart and depend on: Jesus' purpose for coming into the world was to save sinners (1 Timothy 1:15). Jesus saved the world by dying on the cross for our sins; this act brought us to God. This is the kind of life you've been invited into, the kind of life Christ lived. He suffered everything that came his way so you would know that it could be done, and also know how to do it step-by-step. He never did anything wrong. Not once said anything amiss.

They called him every name in the book, and he said nothing back. He suffered through persecution, content to let God set things right. He used his servant body to carry our sins to the cross so we could be rid of sin, free to live the right way. His wounds became your healing. You were a lost sheep with no idea who you were or where you were going. Now you're named and kept for good by the Shepherd of your souls (*1 Peter 2:21-25, The Message*). And because Jesus fulfilled his purpose, three things are offered to all men in the name of Jesus: repentance, remission of sin, and salvation.

- Repentance: act of rejecting sin and returning to God.

Purpose Will Prevail

- Remission of Sins: removal of the guilt or penalty of sin acquired through the belief in Christ.

- Salvation: deliverance from the power of sin; redemption.

Samson: Before Samson came into the world, an angel appeared before his mother and told her she was pregnant with child who would be God's Nazirite from the moment of his birth to his death. God's purpose for Samson was the deliverance of Israel from the Philistines, so He bestowed upon Samson everything that he'd need to carry out this task, including specific instructions and supernatural strength.

And then the People of Israel were back at it again, doing what was evil in God's sight. God put them under the domination of the Philistines for forty years. At that time there was a man named Manoah from Zorah from the tribe of Dan. His wife was barren and childless. The angel of God appeared to her and told her, "I know that you are barren and childless, but you're going to become pregnant and bear a son. But take much care: Drink no wine or beer; eat nothing ritually unclean. You are, in fact, pregnant right now, carrying a son. No razor will touch his head—the boy will be God's Nazirite from the moment of his birth. He will launch the deliverance from Philistine oppression." The woman went to her husband and said, "A man of God came to me. He looked like the angel of God—terror laced with glory! I didn't ask him where he was from and he didn't tell me his name, but he told me, 'You're pregnant. You're going to give birth to a son. Don't drink any wine or beer and eat nothing ritually unclean. The boy will be God's Nazirite from the moment of birth to the day of his death" (Judges 13:1-8, The Message).

Moses: God preserved Moses's life from the time he was born. It was ordered by Pharaoh to put all male children to death: "Everybody that is born you must throw into the Nile, but let every girl live". (Exodus 1:22). Because God had a plan and purpose for Moses, his life was spared. Moses's mother knew there was something special about him, so she hid him for three months. When she could no longer do so, she put him in a basket and put him in the Nile to see what would happen. Pharaoh's daughter saw the child and adopted him. Moses's purpose was to lead the Israelites from captivity in Egypt to salvation in the Promised Land.

A man from the family of Levi married a Levite woman. The woman became pregnant and had a son. She saw there was something special about him and hid him. She hid him for three months. When she couldn't hide him any longer she got a little basket-boat made of papyrus, waterproofed it with tar and pitch, and placed the child in it. Then she set it afloat in the reeds at the edge of the Nile. The baby's older sister found herself a vantage point a little way off and watched to see what would happen to him. Pharaoh's daughter came down to the Nile to bathe; her maidens strolled on the bank. She saw the basket-boat floating in the reeds and sent her maid to get it. She opened it and saw the child—a baby crying! Her heart went out to him. She said, "This must be one of the Hebrew babies." Then his sister was before her: "Do you want me to go and get a nursing

Purpose Will Prevail

mother from the Hebrews so she can nurse the baby for you?" Pharaoh's daughter said, "Yes. Go." The girl went and called the child's mother. Pharaoh's daughter told her, "Take this baby and nurse him for me. I'll pay you." The woman took the child and nursed him. After the child was weaned, she presented him to Pharaoh's daughter who adopted him as her son. She named him Moses (Pulled-Out), saying, "I pulled him out of the water." (Exodus 2:1-10, The Message).

These three men had great and unthinkable destinies that would allow people to see the mighty hand of God. As I look at the life of Jesus, Samson, and Moses, I know I could not fulfill the shoes of these men. This is why God created me for a very unique purpose of my own. Each of these men suffered, but God designed them to handle the path they were on to fulfilling their purpose. Whatever God has created us to do, He designed us with everything we need to fulfill it. I am excited for what God has planned for me. Are you?

You are special to God. He took time out of the equation to create you for such a time as this. We think our parents decided on our name and that it was first pronounced when we were born, but God knew our names before our parents did. Amazing, huh? *But now, thus says the Lord, who created you, O Jacob, And He who formed you, O Israel: "Fear not, for I have redeemed you; I have called you by your name; You are Mine (Isaiah 43:1 NKJV).*

Now let's look *deeper* into purpose. You know that you have a purpose, but how do you activate it? How do you know what it is? How do you start? How do you finish? Before we get into this, there is a problem that needs to be addressed first. Sin! Separation from God. God has a plan and it's all prepared for us, but us being separated from God is a huge hindrance in fulfilling our assignment. Understanding the full effects of sin and how it is used to cause destruction can be tricky to understand at times. It all goes back to the beginning, during the fall of man with the help of a deceiving serpent. Sin has been around for centuries, and, sadly, it is fulfilling the work it was cut out to do. But remember this: God has a plan!

We humans keep brainstorming options and plans, but GOD's purpose prevails (Proverbs 19:21, The Message)

··· *Prayer* ···

Father, in the name of Jesus, I pray that the desire to know you will be greater than before. Father, I pray that those who have a desire to know you will come to the knowledge of who you are. Let this message created specifically for their eyes and ears bring life to their soul and spirit.

Father, reveal to them a greater level of purpose and why they were created. Father, let your unconditional love reach into their hearts and captivate their minds.

In Jesus Name,
Amen

REFLECTIONS

REFLECTIONS

2

Purpose Interrupted

If we confess our sins, He is faithful and just to forgive us our sins and to cleanse us from all unrighteousness

(1John 1:9, NKJV)

Have you ever tasted something so good that you had to taste it again? Eventually, it becomes hard to give up. That's how sin is! It's the main thing that keeps us separated from God. We cannot fulfill our purpose while separated from God. Sin is disobedience that defines and affects our relationship with God. If we continue to sin, we have no real definition of who God is. Sin involves the denial of the living God from whom we draw our life and very existence. It interrupts the plan God has designed for each and every one of us from the foundation of the world. I want to share with you two stories that show just how dangerously effective sin is in us not fulfilling our purpose. Let's examine Genesis 3 and Genesis 4:

The serpent was clever, more clever than any wild animal GOD had made. He spoke to the Woman: "Do I understand that God told you not to eat from any tree in the garden?"

Purpose Will Prevail

The Woman said to the serpent, "Not at all. We can eat from the trees in the garden. It's only about the tree in the middle of the garden that God said, 'Don't eat from it; don't even touch it or you'll die.'"

The serpent told the Woman, "You won't die. God knows that the moment you eat from that tree, you'll see what's really going on. You'll be just like God, knowing everything, ranging all the way from good to evil."

When the Woman saw that the tree looked like good eating and realized what she would get out of it—she'd know everything!—she took and ate the fruit and then gave some to her husband, and he ate.

Immediately the two of them did "see what's really going on"—saw themselves naked! They sewed fig leaves together as makeshift clothes for themselves.

When they heard the sound of GOD strolling in the garden in the evening breeze, the Man and his Wife hid in the trees of the garden, hid from GOD. GOD called to the Man: "Where are you?"

He said, "I heard you in the garden and I was afraid because I was naked. And I hid."

GOD said, "Who told you you were naked? Did you eat from that tree I told you not to eat from?"

The Man said, "The Woman you gave me as a companion, she gave me fruit from the tree, and, yes, I ate it."

GOD said to the Woman, "What is this that you've done?"

Jasma Starks

"The serpent seduced me," she said, "and I ate."

GOD told the serpent:
"Because you've done this, you're cursed,
 cursed beyond all cattle and wild animals,

Cursed to slink on your belly
 and eat dirt all your life.

I'm declaring war between you and the Woman,
 between your offspring and hers.

He'll wound your head,
 you'll wound his heel."

He told the Woman: "I'll multiply your pains in childbirth;
 you'll give birth to your babies in pain.

You'll want to please your husband,
 but he'll lord it over you."

He told the Man: "Because you listened to your wife
 and ate from the tree

That I commanded you not to eat from,
 'Don't eat from this tree,'

The very ground is cursed because of you;
 getting food from the ground

Will be as painful as having babies is for your wife;
 you'll be working in pain all your life long.

Purpose Will Prevail

The ground will sprout thorns and weeds,
 you'll get your food the hard way,

Planting and tilling and harvesting,
 sweating in the fields from dawn to dusk,

Until you return to that ground yourself, dead and buried;
 you started out as dirt, you'll end up dirt."

The Man, known as Adam, named his wife Eve because she was the mother of all the living.

GOD made leather clothing for Adam and his wife and dressed them.

GOD said, "The Man has become like one of us, capable of knowing everything, ranging from good to evil. What if he now should reach out and take fruit from the Tree-of-Life and eat, and live forever? Never—this cannot happen!"

So GOD expelled them from the Garden of Eden and sent them to work the ground, the same dirt out of which they'd been made. He threw them out of the garden and stationed angel-cherubim and a revolving sword of fire east of it, guarding the path to the Tree-of-Life (Genesis 3:1-24, The Message).

Adam and Eve were in the Garden of Eden in the presence of God. God told them bluntly you can eat from whatever tree you want, but do not eat from the tree in the middle of the garden. *GOD commanded the Man, "You can eat from any tree in the garden, except from the Tree-of-Knowledge-of-Good-and-Evil.*

Don't eat from it. The moment you eat from that tree, you're dead (Genesis 2:16-17, The Message). Here comes the deceitful serpent, asking questions. Now Eve is confused, knowing what God told her about the tree; she even repeated it back to the serpent. The serpent twisted what God said, and Eve believed otherwise. She looked at the tree and saw that it looked good, so she ate the fruit off the tree and gave some to Adam. Thus, sin was committed: the act of rebellion or disobedience.

Once the fruit was eaten, Adam and Eve's eyes opened. They then knew the knowledge of good and evil and immediately saw themselves naked, whereas they were not able to tell the difference before. This tells me that the tree was powerful, and it did exactly what God did not want to happen. God came through the garden, and they hid from Him. "Where are you?" God asked. Now whenever God asks a question, He already knows the answer. He just wants us to identify where we are at the current time. Continuing to examine the scriptures, I believe God was asking them where they were *spiritually*. Because after the sin was committed, God felt a difference in the closeness that He shared with them prior to their sin. Remember that God created us in His image, so He knew that His image had been corrupted, which caused the separation. God is holy. Sin isn't a part of His nature, so there had to be consequences for their actions.

Adam and Eve felt the difference in that they were ashamed and hid, and when in the presence of God, you cannot hide. In His presence, everything is exposed. These are two key things to remember. One, you only feel

Purpose Will Prevail

ashamed and withdrawn when you are in sin. Two, this will make you feel unworthy to be in His presence. Consequences included Adam and Eve being removed from the garden and being sent to the ground from which they were made. The serpent was cursed, the ground that man walked on was cursed, and the pain in childbirth multiplied. Everything Adam and Eve needed was in the garden; they wanted for nothing. They were in the presence of God, and when you have a relationship with God, all your needs are met. God even created them to live and not die. Remember, God stated that if they ate from the tree that they would surely die. *You are free to eat from any tree in the garden; but you must not eat from the tree of the knowledge of good and evil, for when you eat from it you will certainly die"(Genesis 2:17, NIV).* Sin gave birth to death. Instead of living eternally, death was brought to the earth, and everything was made temporal.

It is also important to understand that there are two things that will consistently try to keep us from fulfilling our purpose: Satan and self. Why and how do these two things keep us from fulfilling our purpose? Satan is the enemy of God, and he has a plan to stop the plans of God. Satan is out to stop people from fully understanding who God is and what God has for His people. Satan hates when we have a relationship with God because when connected to God, we understand the plans of the enemy and his devices. This is powerful because once we truly understand who we are in God, we have all the power over Satan whose assignment is to stop the plans of God from coming forth. Are you entertaining the plans of Satan or the plans of God?

Pinch yourself. That's the flesh. It's our body, the stuff that wraps around our spirit. It's sinful and loves to feel good. The flesh always desires what is contrary to God and His word. *Romans 8:7-8 states because the carnal mind is enmity against God; for it is not subject to the law of God, nor indeed can be. So then, those who are in the flesh cannot please God (NKJV).* This scripture simply tells us that the flesh cannot please God. We have to learn how to walk in the spirit and control our flesh daily. *I say then: Walk in the Spirit, and you shall not fulfill the lust of the flesh. For the flesh lusts against the Spirit, and the Spirit against the flesh; and these are contrary to one another, so that you do not do the things that you wish. ¹⁸ But if you are led by the Spirit, you are not under the law (Galatians 5:16-18, NKJV).*

Now on to Genesis 4, where Adam and Eve conceived two sons, Cain and Abel:

Adam slept with Eve his wife. She conceived and had Cain. She said, "I've gotten a man, with GOD's help!" Then she had another baby, Abel. Abel was a herdsman and Cain a farmer. Time passed. Cain brought an offering to GOD from the produce of his farm. Abel also brought an offering, but from the firstborn animals of his herd, choice cuts of meat. GOD liked Abel and his offering, but Cain and his offering didn't get his approval. Cain lost his temper and went into a sulk. GOD spoke to Cain: "Why this tantrum? Why the sulking? If you do well, won't you be accepted? And if you don't do well, sin is lying in wait for you, ready to pounce; it's out to get you, you've got to master it." Cain had words with his brother. They were out in the field; Cain came at Abel his brother and killed him. GOD said to Cain, "Where

Purpose Will Prevail

is Abel your brother?" He said, "How should I know? Am I his babysitter?" GOD said, "What have you done! The voice of your brother's blood is calling to me from the ground. From now on you'll get nothing but curses from this ground; you'll be driven from this ground that has opened its arms to receive the blood of your murdered brother. You'll farm this ground, but it will no longer give you its best. You'll be a homeless wanderer on Earth." Cain said to GOD, "My punishment is too much. I can't take it! You've thrown me off the land and I can never again face you. I'm a homeless wanderer on Earth and whoever finds me will kill me (Genesis 4:1-14, The Message).

Let's talk about Cain. He and his brother Abel brought an offering before God. Abel's offering was acceptable, but Cain's was not. Cain got upset and lost his temper, planting jealousy and bitterness in his heart. God warned him that sin desires to have you, but you must rule over it. Cain did not listen, however. He was still upset that his brother brought a better offering to God than he did. Cain purposed it in his heart and mind to kill his brother when he asked him to go out to the field. The Bible states: *For out of the heart proceed evil thoughts, murders, adulteries, fornications, thefts, false witness, blasphemies (Matthew 15:19 NKJV).* When we purpose something in our hearts and let it grow, we allow it into our thoughts, and then it is shown through our actions.

God asked Cain, "Where is Abel, your brother?" Again, God knew the answer, but he asked Cain anyway. Cain acted like he didn't know what happened, so God answered His own question by asking Cain what he had done. "The voice of your brother's blood is calling out to me from the ground." The result of Cain's sin was having to work the ground, yet yielding no crops in doing so. Furthermore, he was doomed to be a restless wanderer on the earth. Cain's response was "Lord my punishment is more than I can bear. Today you are driving me out of the land, and I will be hidden from your presence. I will be a restless wanderer on the earth, and whoever finds me will kill me." God sent Cain to the Land of Nod, east of Eden. Sin is nasty, and a moment of sin can cost you your life and the presence of God.

When Cain stated that his punishment was more than he could bear, he meant he could not imagine his life without God's presence. It is hard to go on with your life without the one who created you. *Nod* is the Hebrew root of the word "to wander." To live in the Land of Nod usually means that one takes up a wandering life. To be separated from God and his presence is to wander. If you are not in a relationship with God, you will wander your whole life. We were created to commune with God daily. His spirit is in us, and God is needed to keep our spirits alive. This is where some of us are now, wandering the earth, thinking we have it all together. If you amount this to having material things and having a job, you are missing the whole point as to why you were created. God has more for us than to live a mediocre life. When we wander, we are living a double-minded life, living in the opinions of others, not knowing which way to go, and searching for something greater, something with meaning. Deep down, we are asking, "Who am I?"

Purpose Will Prevail

I understand, and I am in no way exempted from sin. But once I found out who God really was and what He wanted for me, it blew my mind. I had to change. There was a time in my life that I let sin attach itself to me. And when I got deep in sin, it was so hard to get out. My spirit yearned for God, but my flesh got what it wanted which was to feel good. The deeper I was in sin, the further I moved away from God. I was trying to make life work on my own terms, apart from what God had for me. Let me tell you, it will not work. I was like Cain. I was spiritually wandering, my mind was wandering, and it was like I was going in circles. I am so happy to share with you that there is hope, there is freedom, and there is a way out of the Land of Nod. Do you want out? *For all have sinned and fall short of the glory of God (Romans 3:23, NKJV).*

Only one of us is perfect, and that is our savior, Jesus Christ. That was the whole purpose of Jesus coming into the world. When we come to acknowledge that we are sinners and that, through repentance, we are saved and redeemed, only then will our divine purpose be activated inside of us. Are you ready to activate your God-given purpose? Jesus is one of the greatest people I know that walked the face of this earth unashamed, powerful, and in authority. He lived his purpose so that we can live ours.

Prayer

Father, in the name of Jesus, I pray that something was shaken and stirred in the heart of the reader to forsake sin and follow you. Father, may our hearts have a yearning to seek after you in all that we do. Father, right now in the name of Jesus, if there be anything that will try to interrupt the plan or purpose of God for our life, I bind it now and destroy its purpose. Father, let us not look to self, but let us look to you for answers that will fulfill our purpose. Father, give us the strength to walk away from sin and live right. I loose the blood of Jesus to cover our minds and deplete the voice of the enemy.

In Jesus Name,
Amen

REFLECTIONS

REFLECTIONS

3

Purpose Activated

Being confident of this very thing, that He who has begun a good work in you will complete it until the day of Jesus Christ

(Philippians 1:6, NKJV)

Jesus was the only man who walked the face of the earth and didn't sin. Jesus is our example that it can be done, no matter the circumstance. Because sin separates us from our Heavenly Father, God used Jesus to bring us back into covenant with Him.

For this reason Christ is the mediator of a new covenant, that those who are called may receive the promised eternal inheritance—now that he has died as a ransom to set them free from the sins committed under the first covenant (Hebrews 9:15, NIV).

Before Jesus could fulfill his purpose, he had to go through a process that would equip, teach, and help every person on earth fulfill their purpose. Before Jesus was born, we know that it was prophesied that he was coming by way of a virgin. Mary, a virgin, had given birth to a Son, and named him Jesus.

Purpose Will Prevail

Now the birth of Jesus Christ took place in this way. When his mother Mary had been betrothed to Joseph, before they came together she was found to be with child from the Holy Spirit. And her husband Joseph, being a just man and unwilling to put her to shame, resolved to divorce her quietly. But as he considered these things, behold, an angel of the Lord appeared to him in a dream, saying, "Joseph, son of David, do not fear to take Mary as your wife, for that which is conceived in her is from the Holy Spirit. She will bear a son, and you shall call his name Jesus, for he will save his people from their sins." All this took place to fulfill what the Lord had spoken by the prophet: "Behold, the virgin shall conceive and bear a son, and they shall call his name Immanuel" which means, God with us (Matthew 1:18-23, NKJV).

Now it is stated in Luke 3:23 that Jesus began his ministry at about thirty years old, and his ministry lasted three years. Whenever God has a plan for us to do something, He also has a timeframe in mind. This tells us that Jesus was in preparation for his purpose. He was in training, getting equipped for what he was designed for. It is important that we prepare ourselves for our assignment. Jesus made himself available to God; he spent time with God as one of his primary tactics of getting ready to fulfill his assignment.

Every year Jesus' parents went to Jerusalem for the Festival of the Passover. When he was twelve years old, they went up to the festival, according to the custom. After the festival was over, while his parents were returning home, the boy Jesus stayed behind in Jerusalem, but they were unaware of it. Thinking he was in their company, they traveled on for a day. Then they began looking for him among their relatives and friends. When they did not find him, they went back to Jerusalem to look for him. After three days they found him in the temple courts, sitting among the teachers, listening to them and asking them questions. Everyone who heard him was amazed at his understanding and his answers. When his parents saw him, they were astonished. His mother said to him, "Son, why have you treated us like this? Your father and I have been anxiously searching for you (Luke 2: 41-48, NIV)."

Jesus was going through the process of purpose; God was preparing him for what was to come. His purpose was unfolding, and he was walking in it. When Jesus started his ministry, he gave it everything he had with no turning back. At the beginning of Jesus's ministry, the devil came to tempt him after fasting forty days and forty nights. *The devil said to him, "If you are the Son of God, tell this stone to become bread" (Luke 4:3, NIV).* Whenever we start to walk in our purpose and fulfill what God has designed for us to do, the enemy always tries to knock us off course and deceive us. No matter what the enemy threw in the face of Jesus, he overcame it by the Word of God. When Jesus didn't give into the temptation of the devil, the devil left him alone. It is important on our journey with God that we resist the devil and speak the Word of God.

Jesus is one of a kind; he is full of power and authority. He is unique, and there is no one like him in the land. People are astonished by the anointing, the power, and the gift that is on his life. Jesus was a teacher, preacher,

Purpose Will Prevail

motivational speaker, and life coach. You name it, and Jesus did it. He had power that the human mind could not comprehend. He healed the sick, drove out evil spirits, trained and developed leaders, and broke traditions and religious mindsets. He calmed storms, raised people from the dead, forgave sins, fed thousands, and performed miracles of every kind. I can go on and on about what Jesus did. Walking out this outstanding purpose, I think I would have needed thirty years of preparation too. Jesus is a mind blower. He stepped on a lot of toes, but he was fulfilling his purpose with God's direction, and not through the opinions of others.

Then the time had come. Jesus had laid the foundational work for his purpose to come to pass. He had family, his disciples, and other people that loved him dearly. Jesus predicted his own death to people who knew him but didn't want to believe what he was saying. *From that time on Jesus began to explain to his disciples that he must go to Jerusalem and suffer many things at the hands of the elders, the chief priests and the teachers of the law, and that he must be killed and on the third day be raised to life.*

Peter took him aside and began to rebuke him. "Never, Lord!" he said. "This shall never happen to you!" Jesus turned and said to Peter, "Get behind me, Satan! You are a stumbling block to me; you do not have in mind the concerns of God, but merely human concerns."

Then Jesus said to his disciples, "Whoever wants to be my disciple must deny themselves and take up their cross and follow me. For whoever wants to save their life will lose it, but whoever loses their life for me will find it. What good will it be for someone to gain the whole world, yet forfeit their soul? Or what can anyone give in exchange for their soul? For the Son of Man is going to come in his Father's glory with his angels, and then he will reward each person according to what they have done. "Truly I tell you, some who are standing here will not taste death before they see the Son of Man coming in his kingdom (Matthew 16:21-28, NIV)."

If you knew you were going to die, wouldn't you do everything in your power to reverse whatever you needed to in order to live? I know! I would too, but Jesus couldn't. It was predestined for him. Your purpose is yours. No one else could live your life and walk in your shoes—only you. Are you willing to walk your purpose out no matter what? Jesus was, even though sometimes he asked God, "Lord can this cup be passed from me?" (*Matthew26:39, NKJV*). Jesus also responded, "Not my will, but your will be done." Because he had a purpose that was beyond his physical capability to complete, he needed God, his father, to get through the process. God had anointed him and given him power for the journey. Jesus was our human example of God, the Father. Even though Jesus had power to do anything, he had to walk through the process to show us the way.

Jesus was betrayed by some close to him, but let it happen because he knew it was a part of the plan. Certain people are in your life for a reason, unintentionally and intentionally placed to help you fulfill your purpose. Then some people are placed by the enemy; this would be

Purpose Will Prevail

unintentionally. And some are intentionally placed by God. Be able to discern the difference. The betrayal got Jesus arrested and crucified.

Now from the sixth hour until the ninth hour there was darkness over all the land. And about the ninth hour Jesus cried out with a loud voice, saying, "Eli, Eli, lama sabachthani?" that is, "My God, My God, why have You forsaken Me?" Some of those who stood there, when they heard that, said, "This Man is calling for Elijah!" Immediately one of them ran and took a sponge, filled it with sour wine and put it on a reed, and offered it to Him to drink. The rest said, "Let Him alone; let us see if Elijah will come to save Him." And Jesus cried out again with a loud voice, and yielded up His spirit. Then, behold, the veil of the temple was torn in two from top to bottom; and the earth quaked, and the rocks were split, ⁵² and the graves were opened; and many bodies of the saints who had fallen asleep were raised; ⁵³ and coming out of the graves after His resurrection, they went into the holy city and appeared to many. So when the centurion and those with him, who were guarding Jesus, saw the earthquake and the things that had happened, they feared greatly, saying, "Truly this was the Son of God!" And many women who followed Jesus from Galilee, ministering to Him, were there looking on from afar, ⁵⁶ among whom were Mary Magdalene, Mary the mother of James and Joses, and the mother of Zebedee's sons (Matthew 27: 45-56, NKJV).

Who would give up their life for yours? Give up their life so that you can live, and live in freedom? There are not too many people we know who will brutally die for us. As I think about Jesus and his final hours on earth, it breaks my heart to know the pain and agony he went through for us. All while being nailed to the cross, he had us, mankind, in mind. Jesus was buried and rose from the dead on the third day. I don't know about you, but this excites me. Because when Jesus got up, my purpose was restored. The life, death, burial, and resurrection are very crucial to fulfilling your purpose on earth. We are also capable of carrying out those marvelous works that he did. In fact, he said that we would do even greater things! Jesus has restored our power, authority, dominion, and purpose to invade the earth. If you can imagine the things that Jesus did, imagine yourself doing that and much, much more. When I say you were created for a great work, believe me, you were created for something beyond human comprehension. Because of the weightiness and uniqueness of your purpose, you have to go to God for the pieces of the puzzle.

Very truly I tell you, whoever believes in me will do the works I have been doing, and they will do even greater things than these, because I am going to the Father (John 14:12, NIV).

I am excited that you got to experience the life of Jesus with me and how he left a great legacy for us to pick up and continue, for us to add to the legacy. What type of legacy do you want to leave behind? Would you like to know this Jesus and how to get in alignment with his word to answer the call and purpose he has for your life? God is a loving God and no matter the sin you have committed, or how great the sin is, He is a forgiver. He is waiting with arms wide open to receive you into His kingdom. One of the mistakes we make is trying to get ourselves together before we come to Jesus, but come to him as you are, and he will make you new.

Would you like to accept Jesus Christ into your heart today? Repeat after me: Jesus, thank you for dying on the cross for my sins. I confess with my mouth that you, Jesus Christ, are Lord. And I believe with my all heart that you died and rose on the third day. Wash me clean; make me new, so that I can live big for you.

You are saved now! All of the angels in heaven are rejoicing. Stop for a second and make this time personal with the Lord. Let Jesus minister to your heart and spirit.

I tell you that in the same way there will be more rejoicing in heaven over one sinner who repents than over ninety-nine righteous persons who do not need to repent (Luke 15:7, NIV).

If you declare with your mouth, "Jesus is Lord," and believe in your heart that God raised him from the dead, you will be saved. (Romans 10:9, NIV).

Stay with me as I get to the nitty gritty. Before purpose can be born or released, there is a process. Many of us despise the process because of the pain and pressure. Oh, but it is oh so worth the end result. Did you know that sometimes you are your worst enemy when it comes to walking in your purpose? If you understood the process, you would embrace it.

...Prayer...

Father, I thank you for those who have accepted your son, Jesus Christ as their Lord and Savior. Father, have your way in their life. Let your divine will be done for their lives. Father, show yourself strong and mighty in their life. Father, reveal to them their purpose and assignment; reveal to them why you created them. Father, I cover them with the blood of Jesus, and loose a hedge of protection to cover their life. Let the power of the Holy Spirit rest heavily on them. Father, prepare their hearts and minds for a great journey in you.

In Jesus Name,
Amen

REFLECTIONS

REFLECTIONS

4

The Process of Purpose

*I'm not saying that I have this all together, that I have it made. But I am well on my way, reaching out for Christ, who has so wondrously reached out for me.
Friends, don't get me wrong: By no means do I count myself an expert in all of this, but I've got my eye on the goal, where God is beckoning us onward—to Jesus. I'm off and running, and I'm not turning back*

(Philippians 3: 12-14, Message)

Often times we do not understand the process of purpose, or we get afraid of the process and quit before we ever reach our purpose. The following analogy will help you understand the process and will cause you to look at every situation in your life differently. It will also allow you to identify what stage you are in. There is a process to everything in life. Without it, how can we ever succeed in anything?

The natural birthing process is very much similar to the spiritual birthing process, yet very different. Both are complex in nature, but before the birthing process can begin, there has to be a pregnancy. God has allowed me to understand the spiritual birthing process from a natural standpoint. *1 Corinthians 15:46, states that the spiritual did not come first, but the natural, and after that the spiritual (NIV).* In order for us to understand spiritual things, we must first understand the natural. If you are a male reading this book, keep going. The birthing process is meant for you as well. *There is neither Jew nor Gentile, neither slave nor free, nor is there male and female, for you are all one in Christ Jesus (Galatians 3:28, NIV).* The natural birthing analogy is just a way for you to understand how the process happens in the spirit. We know, in the natural, that only women can become pregnant and give birth. A woman and a man must become intimate to conceive a baby. After a man releases his sperm, it has to come into contact with a woman's egg. If the egg meets up with a healthy sperm on its way to the uterus, the process of creating new life begins. Now to the spiritual!

If you declare with your mouth, "Jesus is Lord," and believe in your heart that God raised him from the dead, you will be saved (Romans 10:9, NIV). After you accept Jesus Christ into your life as Lord and Savior, there is more to it than just going to heaven. You have work to do! We all have a purpose that must be fulfilled in the earth. How do we know what our purpose is? After accepting Christ, we become a new creation in him. *Therefore, if anyone is in Christ, the new creation has come: The old has gone, the new is here! (2 Corinthians 5:17, NIV).* In becoming a new creation in Christ, we then desire the things of Christ. One of the first things we desire is to know Christ intimately, and one of the ways of becoming intimate with Christ is through worship. Yes, worship. Worship is when we deny any other god or idol. We spend time with the Lord, and His presence consumes our entire being. *For in him we live, and move, and have our being (Acts 17:28, NIV).*

Worship is a lifestyle; our entire persona lives and represents the image of God. Persona means the role or character adopted by an author or an actor. When we worship God and spend time with Him, we begin to put on His character. *He predestined us for adoption to sonship through Jesus Christ, in accordance with his pleasure and will (Ephesians 1:5, NIV).* When you are adopted into a family, you put on the characteristics of that family. This is why we must become imitators of God. This is why it is stated in the Word of God to worship the Lord thy God only. *Jesus answered, "It is written: 'Worship the Lord your God and serve him only (Luke 4:8, NIV).'"* When we worship God and spend time with Him, we love on Him; we express reverence and adoration for Him. We begin to glorify Him—exalt, honor, and magnify Him. This is when the intimacy happens. The key is that we must learn to spend time with God and stay in His presence. Here, God loves on us back and reminds us how wonderful we are. When God loves on us, it is better than any manmade love. It is the love of the Heavenly Father! In the midst of intimacy with the Father, purpose is conceived.

If you have not accepted Jesus Christ as Lord and Savior over your life, it is hard to conceive the promises of God for your life. If you don't worship the true and living God, there is only one other person who thinks he is God, and that is Satan. From the minute we were born, Satan was

Purpose Will Prevail

out to kill, steal, and destroy because he knew that you had a great assignment on your life. If we do not worship God, we worship Satan. As stated above, to worship someone or something is to reverence them, exalt them, and spend time with them. If you are worshiping Satan, you can also conceive, but it will not be the promises of God. The only thing you will conceive is sin and death.

The Bible declares in James 1:15, *Then, after desire has conceived, it gives birth to sin; and sin, when it is full-grown, gives birth to death (NIV)*. Being a good person is not good enough. I'm sorry, that doesn't cut it. Good people worship Satan too. How, you ask? There is only one God; there is none above or beside Him. As people, we long to worship something because that is how we were created. Please hear my heart. Satan is a deceiver, and it is his job to distract us and focus our attention on other things. The number one thing we do as humans is create idols to worship, gravitating toward anything that gives us a sense of power (e.g., money, people, cars, pornography, etc.). In Exodus 32: 1-8, the Israelites built themselves an idol and God was not pleased. *Now when the people saw that Moses delayed coming down from the mountain, the people gathered together to Aaron, and said to him, "Come, and make us gods that shall go before us; for as for this Moses, the man who brought us up out of the land of Egypt, we do not know what has become of him." And Aaron said to them, "Break off the golden earrings which are in the ears of your wives, your sons, and your daughters, and bring them to me." So all the people broke off the golden earrings which were in their ears, and brought them to Aaron. And he received the gold from their hand, and he fashioned it with an engraving tool, and made a molded calf. Then they said, "This is your god, O Israel, that brought you out of the land of Egypt!"*

So when Aaron saw it, he built an altar before it. And Aaron made a proclamation and said, "Tomorrow is a feast to the LORD." Then they rose early on the next day, offered burnt offerings, and brought peace offerings; and the people sat down to eat and drink, and rose up to play.

And the LORD said to Moses, "Go, get down! For your people whom you brought out of the land of Egypt have corrupted themselves. They have turned aside quickly out of the way which I commanded them. They have made themselves a molded calf, and worshiped it and sacrificed to it, and said, 'This is your god, O Israel, that brought you out of the land of Egypt!'" (NKJV)

Let's not be ignorant of the enemy and his devices. He wants us to believe that we do not need Jesus and can make it in this world without him. That is a straight lie from the pit of hell! *Lest Satan should get an advantage of us: for we are not ignorant of his devices (2 Corinthians 2:11, NKJV).*

••• Pregnant with Purpose

After conception, now you are pregnant with purpose. What's next? What does it mean to be pregnant with purpose? It means that God has placed something inside of your spirit that needs to be birthed into the world. For example, when we spend time with God, all of a sudden we get ideas, visions, and images of things He wants us to

Purpose Will Prevail

build and birth. Oftentimes I'll be in the presence of God and will have a vision of me doing something, and I'm taken aback. *Lord, you trust me with this?* The idea is so big, I think, Lord, there is no way this vision will be fulfilled without you.

Okay, back to the natural! We understand that once a woman conceives she is pregnant. She has nine months to carry a baby, which are broken into three trimesters. The number nine symbolizes divine completion, or conveys the meaning of finality. The first trimester is one of the toughest because the woman's body is going through changes to be able to hold the fetus for nine months. Those first three months present the greatest threat. Most women are excited to tell everyone that they are pregnant, but that is not one of the smartest things to do because the first trimester is a vulnerable stage for the baby and the mother.

When I conceived my first child, I told everyone as soon as I found out. Weeks later, on Valentine's Day, I went to the doctor to see and hear the heartbeat. The anticipation was nerve-racking. I'd waited all the week and all day for that moment, and there it was...*nothing*. There was no baby. My heart filled with sadness and grief as to why this was happening to me. The sac started forming, and, somewhere along the way, the baby aborted itself. Now this may have happened for many reasons, but my heart didn't care. I was supposed to have a baby. For the women who have had a miscarriage before, you have learned from the first time not to open your mouth until you have passed the first trimester; it is a sign of hope that the process will be fulfilled. The chance of miscarriage significantly drops after the first three months. Afterwards, you still only tell a select amount of people, and then when it is noticeable, people will see it for themselves.

Pregnancy is different for every woman. We will not all have the same symptoms and struggles. However, we all need a doctor throughout the whole pregnancy. There is no way you will be able to go through your pregnancy without any guidance. The doctor is the expert in this area. They have the discernment to see and catch things that you will not be able to see because they are trained in this area. Instructions are given on how to maintain a healthy pregnancy, and the doctor also records and collects information to see if there will be any difficulty in the pregnancy that can be prevented, including:

- The woman's due date.
- The health history.
- The medical history of family members.
- Risk factors based on age, health and/or personal and family history.

All of this is necessary to determine the process of the pregnancy. The doctor prescribes prenatal vitamins, along with other specific instructions, including diet and exercise, to help with the health and nutrition of the baby. You can no longer do and eat some of the things you once did.

Purpose Will Prevail

Likewise, there are also stages in being pregnant with purpose. Once God has impregnated us with our divine mission, we are excited. We want to share with everyone what God has placed inside of us to birth and accomplish. Let me caution you: Do not do it. It is not for everybody to hear. The minute you open your mouth, be ready for others' opinions to hit you like a whirlwind. When you speak of your purpose before it is time, you have to fight more than what the process calls for.

The enemy doesn't know your assignment given to you by God. He knows that you have a great assignment on your life, but only until you open your mouth does he know what it is. When he knows your assignment, he tries to gather a plan and put the best devices together to be a hindrance. This is a very vulnerable stage for the believer as well. As important as it is for a woman to see a doctor throughout her entire pregnancy, it is equally important in the spirit. You need Jesus Christ throughout your whole pregnancy, throughout your whole life. We serve a blesser, so this means you will be pregnant many times with plans for the Lord. If we are not willing to give up our sinful nature, this can have a negative effect on the purpose we carry inside of us. The chances of a miscarriage are high; it is when we put off the sinful nature that we will be safe in Christ. *You were taught, with regard to your former way of life, to put off your old self, which is being corrupted by its deceitful desires; to be made new in the attitude of your minds; and to put on the new self, created to be like God in true righteousness and holiness (Ephesians 4:22-24, NIV).*

As the doctor has instructions for a pregnant woman to stay healthy, God has instructions for His children to stay holy. *Walk in obedience to all that the LORD your God has commanded you, so that you may live and prosper and prolong your days in the land that you will possess (Deuteronomy 5:33, NIV).* As every pregnancy is different, so is the walk of each believer. We will all go through different trials, tests, and tribulations; they are there to make us stronger. *Consider it pure joy, my brothers and sisters, whenever you face trials of many kinds, because you know that the testing of your faith produces perseverance. Let perseverance finish its work so that you may be mature and complete, not lacking anything. (James 1:2-4, NIV).*

Just as the doctor prescribes prenatal pills to a pregnant woman, God also prescribes instructions for His children. We know them, but do we exercise them? Read your Bible, pray, praise, give thanks, worship, meditate, declare, fast, etc. The same way you conceived and activated purpose is the same way you keep it—in worship, in the presence of God. Jesus Christ is the expert on birthing purpose. He is the promise maker, and he placed the purpose in your spirit. What better person to go to for instruction than the one who created it, majors in it, and sustains it?

The natural pregnancy stage is nine months. Sometimes the baby comes earlier, or even after the due date. The spiritual birthing stage is different because God's timing is different from the natural sense. God's timing can be anywhere from two months to ten years and beyond. Your birthing time is determined by how great your divine purpose is. Your obedience also plays an essential role to

Purpose Will Prevail

birthing in God's timing. It is important to know some history of your family. Ask God to show you what your family had to deal with when carrying great purpose such as ideas, inventions, business concepts, etc. For believers, this could be generational curses, things that are in the bloodline. What demons/spirits did family members have to fight and overcome? I am referring to spirits like depression, fear, procrastination, doubt, unbelief, and so forth. If these spirits are not dealt with, how will it affect your purpose, pregnancy and birthing process? God has given us the authority to cast down every spirit of the enemy that will try to distract us from fulfilling the purposes of God on our life. *Behold, I give unto you power to tread on serpents and scorpions, and over all the power of the enemy: and nothing shall by any means hurt you (Luke 10:19, NKJV).*

I do not want to make this about religion, but relationship. I cannot express how important it is to have covering such as a pastor or mentor when walking out your purpose. This trusted guide will be able to cover you and train you in fulfilling your purpose. There must be guidance and accountability. You need trustworthy and empowering people to help you propel forward.

The second trimester is usually the easiest. Again, it depends on the woman, her body and how she is adapting to the changes. For some women, morning sickness has stopped and you can eat a little more than you did in the first trimester. This is one of the happiest stages because the couple learns the gender of their baby and can begin preparing for what the baby needs. The child's life is also sometimes celebrated through baby showers.

At this time, in the spiritual stage, God will give us a taste of what He has placed inside of us. If He gives us full details of the process, we wouldn't finish. Walking with the Lord is not always easy, but the believer always comes out on top. *For we live by faith, not by sight (2 Corinthians 5:7, NIV).* This is why the bible tells us, *Trust in the Lord with all your heart and lean not on your own understanding; in all your ways submit to him, and he will make your paths straight (Proverbs 3:5-6, NIV).*

In the process of fulfilling our purpose, God equips us for the great birthing, and because every believer's walk is different, God will have us do different stuff to prepare us and test our obedience. For an example, if God has placed an idea for a business in your spirit, you cannot just start selling products; you have to go through the process. Does this business require you to have a degree? Do you need liability insurance? Will you be a for-profit or a nonprofit business? What is your mission and vision? What is the company's name? These are processes that you cannot miss in birthing a business. If any steps are missed, it'll affect the outcome.

Being confident of this, that he who began a good work in you will carry it on to completion until the day of Christ Jesus (Philippians 1:6, NIV).

The third trimester is the last and most uncomfortable stage in pregnancy. The body is preparing itself to deliver the baby, so the baby is positioning himself to be born (usually head down). At this stage, the doctor orders bed rest if the mother is dilating too early. The baby needs to stay in the womb until he is fully developed. This is also the stage where the pain comes. It seems like no matter what the mother does to get comfortable, it doesn't work.

Out of the whole pregnancy, the birthing process is the most painful. Once the sharp pains kick in, the baby is closer to making an entrance into the world. It's time! The doctor is called, and the mother is rushed to the emergency room to give birth. The birthing processes are as different as the pregnancies themselves. Some women get an epidural to help with the pain; others don't.

The pain is almost more than she can bear, but she knows the gift she is about to birth is going to change her life. Women make different sounds when birthing the baby because of the pain. *Birth Plans for Dummies* states that moaning and groaning during child birth is normal and natural. This instinctual reaction to contractions and the baby's movements has a soothing effect. The vibrations of the mother's voice reverberates through her body while the sound fills her ears with a calming tone. During the pushing phase, moaning and groaning can help the mother push instinctually, almost guiding and encouraging her muscles to bear down in just the right way.

The baby's head is down, and the mother is pushing and pushing. She can feel the pressure, but she is determined to push the baby out despite the pain. Hours later, the baby is out and the mother is embracing her miracle. A woman was created to give birth. It's one of her many purposes. This is the part that blows my mind: When the baby is born, the mother forgets the pain she went through just moments ago. The baby she birthed is much greater than the pain she experienced.

We are in pain, pregnant with purpose. It's time to PUSH. The pain seems more than we can bear. We are asking God why me, what is going on, what did I do wrong? You start to doubt a little bit, but you know in your heart what God told you, yet you're saying this can't be God. It's okay. It's a part of the birthing process. When it's time to PUSH, get into position to pray; watch how your voice changes. Oftentimes when I am in prayer, I moan and groan because the pressure hurts. God hears and says it's time, get into your birthing position and push. Pray! We birth that purpose God has placed in us, and we cannot even begin to explain that joy we feel for the baby we have birthed. Instantly, the pain ceases, and we are amazed at what God birthed. Do not underestimate the baby you are pregnant with. It will blow your mind. Are you ready to give birth to that purpose that is placed inside of you? I am!

I have laid the foundation for you to understand purpose using an analysis of Jesus's life and an analogy of the birthing process. Now I want to give you something more tangible that will get to the core of your heart and spirit. I want to give you *me*—the truth about me, the naked truth. It's not easy uncovering myself, but I want to show you how, from the beginning I was created for greatness, and how sin, myself, and Satan tried to interrupt the plans God

Purpose Will Prevail

had for my life. I want to show you how real God is, and how He can transform your life if you only believe. Take this journey with me. Do me a favor. Get real with yourself, and get real with God. Who are you *really*? Are you living who He created you to be? The unexpected of my life unfolds.

... Prayer ...

Father, in the name of Jesus, thank you for the process of purpose, even though it may be hard sometimes to endure the pain and the pressure. Keep us as we walk through this journey with you. Thank you for trusting us with such great promises. Father, when we feel like giving up, give us strength for the journey. Let our process of purpose be a testimony to someone else to help them fulfill their purpose.

In Jesus Name,
Amen

REFLECTIONS

REFLECTIONS

5

The Unexpected: My Testimony

And they overcame him by the blood of the Lamb and by the word of their testimony, and they did not love their lives to the death

(Revelation 12:11, NKJV).

My heart pounded as I looked out the window of that big yellow school bus. I became very anxious to see who would pick me up from the bus stop. I wanted it to be anybody but the man who exposed me to the life of my sexuality before it was time. My aunt's husband planted a seed that would change my life. My aunt had to work all the time, so the responsibility was left to her husband to pick me up from the bus stop. I was left alone with a man who was perverted in his mind and would do anything to get his desires met as a man.

As I tell this story, it is becoming so clear of how afraid I was. Afraid that a man three times my size would hurt me. He distorted my view of relationships and what they should look like. He distorted my view of what marriage should look like. He distorted my view of sex and how it was meant to be for the husband and wife.

Purpose Will Prevail

I remember being in a bedroom, feeling ashamed and silenced, confused about what was going on. I laid in bed as a grown man touched me for his pleasure and made me touch him; this was an ongoing activity for a while. Molestation became a part of who I was, and I was told that if I said anything, my family would get hurt. Being a child, I didn't understand what was going on and why this was happening to me. So I kept quiet, and feelings of hopelessness and shame attached themselves to my spirit. I was only five years old. Where was my family when this man hurt my heart? When this man used my innocence to keep a secret? Where was God? These are all questions I began to ask myself. The molestation eventually stopped, but the hurt and the images in my head lived on. I never told a soul what happened to me until my teenage years.

Years later, I was still young, but I knew I was created for a purpose. I knew that God had a great calling for my life. God was speaking to me and showing me little nuggets of what I was created for. I would seek out guidance from others around me so that I could fully understand what was happening in my life, and I would do this by going to church and getting around people of the same faith who could nurture the things of God that were developing inside of me. I wanted to know how to get to know this God who was speaking to me. I began to pray on my own with the guidance from God, and for years I prayed nothing but the Lord's Prayer.

In this manner, therefore, pray:

Our Father in heaven,
Hallowed be your name.
Your kingdom come.
Your will be done
On earth as it is in heaven.
Give us this day our daily bread.
And forgive us our debts,
as we forgive our debtors.
And do not lead us into temptation,
but deliver us from the evil one.
For Yours is the kingdom and the power and the glory
forever. Amen (Matthew 6:9-13, NKJV).

This prayer consumed my very being. I couldn't go to sleep without praying. If I did, I woke up to pray. Prayer was my life! At a young age, God was preparing me to be an intercessor, a prayer warrior. He was preparing and teaching me how to pray, and then I started reading His word. I thank my mother for reading her bible daily without skipping a beat. She was my example that the Word of God was effective for living a righteous and purpose-filled life. I began to go to church with some friends, confessed my sins, let Jesus Christ into my heart, and was baptized.

At the very beginning of my life, there was already an assignment set out to destroy my destiny. Nobody chooses for bad things to happen to them, but they do. We have to understand whatever happens to us does not define who we are. But the very thing that happened to me at a very young age was about to resurface. The residue of sexual sin had attached itself to my life. It was the plan of the enemy to keep me in bondage and hold me captive in my mind. God also revealed to me that this was a generational curse that had been held in my family's bloodline for years. In eighth grade, I became curious about sex and began to play around with the idea. I knew it was wrong, but I was trapped and didn't know how to get out. There were so many chances I had to lose my virginity, but I was so scared of the consequence. I was scared of giving myself to someone. Would I feel that same feeling I felt when I was molested?

I was only in eighth grade, so why was I interested in sex? Why was I so anxious and curious of the very thing that could shatter my heart and tie my soul? This whole time, I had been going back and forth. There was a fight between my flesh and spirit. I wanted to do what was right, but I had no control over my flesh. From the minute you are born, you are always in preparation for your purpose. Our parents are supposed to guide us and teach us the way until we are able to make decisions of our own. I didn't grow up in the traditional Christian home and wasn't taught to follow Christ. God gave me a yearning to follow Him. Watching my mother read her bible everyday sparked an interest in my heart to know and understand what she was reading. However, my parents didn't speak to me about Christ, and there were no set disciplines or principles to follow a Christian lifestyle. God gave me the yearning to have a deeper revelation of Him, so I began to seek Him out on my own.

High school was tough. I was looking for love and wanting to experience love, but I had no idea what love was. I thought that love would fill voids in my heart or take away the curiosity that I felt, but the enemy set a trap I couldn't resist. When you are living for God, the enemy sets traps that look extra good; he gives you everything you want. If you like chocolate, he won't give you vanilla, he'll give you chocolate. The very thing we think we need is sent to harm us, not help us. I met this guy, and he was everything that attracted me to a male. He said *one* thing to me, and that was it. I fell hard! A couple months later, I lost my virginity. I gave him my soul, I gave him *me*. I created a soul tie that I could not easily give up or break.

When I became intimate with this person, I attracted and received everything he was dealing with. We have to be careful who we lay down with; we have no idea what they are dealing with. The thing is, I attracted him. Lust saw lust and started mingling. My spirit was defiled; flesh was getting the glory instead of God. A soul tie is dangerous if you are not married. Satan takes advantage of ungodly soul ties. There can be a transfer of spirits from one person to another. Sleep with someone who is not your husband or wife, and all of sudden you start dealing with stuff you never had to deal with before. This soul tie had me in bondage. I was doing stuff I had no business doing or had desired to do before.

Although I did everything I could to make him happy, he was extremely mean to me. There was no changing this situation; I was extremely hurt and miserable. I didn't know what to do but go to God. My spirit wanted out of the relationship, but my flesh was satisfied with sin. My flesh was okay with being separated from God.

Purpose Will Prevail

I had gone to an appointment at the doctor's office. I don't know what happened, but I ended up passing out, and when I woke up I was being asked 101 questions. The question I dreaded had been asked. Are you sexually active? My mother was staring me dead in the face. I wanted to lie so bad, but I didn't know what the results of the blood test would be, so I told the truth. My mother looked at me with tears in her eyes before snatching a necklace off my neck she had given me. Her words were, *"I don't want you to be like me."* My mother had children young and worked very hard to support us and ensure we had the best life. I understood what she meant, and her words cut me to the core. I didn't want to hurt her or anybody else anymore. After a week of waiting, everything was fine. I wasn't pregnant; I was just shook up and scared as hell.

After this encounter at the doctor's office I finally got the courage to tell my family what had happened to me as a little girl. The look of hurt on my family's face as they gathered around to hear what I had to say was a hard pill to swallow, but the healing process had finally begun. It was as if a weight had been lifted.

I was so tired of doing things my way. I wanted out of this sin that held me down. I asked a friend a question that would change my life: Can I go to church with you? I went to church the following Sunday and had a supernatural encounter with God. He spoke to my heart and said that He loved me. Those words changed my life. I had repented for the sin I committed. I became sold out for Christ. My time with God increased; His word was in my heart and mouth. I began praying and coming out of a dark place in my life, ministering for the Lord, and bringing people to Christ. Satan decided he was going to hit me another way since I had decided to give up sexual sin.

Little did Satan know, what he had planned would only make me stronger. What's the closest thing to a person? Their family! I have two particular brothers that were caught up in gangs. I remember thinking if God didn't protect them, either they or someone close to them were going to die. God used their situation to train me how to pray against demons that have been sent to destroy. I had that feeling that if I didn't pray, somebody was going to die. At this time in my life, God had given me dreams. It amazed me. I would have dreams of things happening that would actually come true. I would wonder what type of gift that was, but it was God's way of speaking to me and letting me know what was going to happen before it did. If it was bad, I could pray against the plan of the enemy or whatever God told me to pray. My brothers were into selling drugs, not seeing how it affected their family. Our house was shot up by gangs, and both of my brothers have been back and forth from jail. One was actually shot, but thank God for His protection, he lived. Our house had been raided and flipped upside down. One of the reasons God created me was to be a deliverer for my family and lead them to Jesus, the ultimate deliverer, so that they can know Christ and walk in their purpose.

Whenever the enemy sees you living godly, his ultimate purpose is to stop you from living that life. I decided to go to college to pursue education and met another guy, but

Purpose Will Prevail

this time was different. I had been in the presence of the Lord, and I was attracted to his spirit. I was attracted to the fact that he worshiped God unashamed. Like me, he was saved. I had finally attracted someone who was attracted to my spirit, the good in me. We talked and chose to become friends. We later dated and married two years later. I was twenty years old when I got married. I didn't care what anybody had to say about it. I didn't care if I was young. This was who I married and loved. Our pasts didn't matter to each other.

I got married without dealing with deeply rooted issues. This caused a problem for the newlywed couple. Sure, my husband had problems too, but I had stuff so deeply rooted that marriage only magnified it. The first year or two of marriage went great. My ego blew up, and I became very prideful; you couldn't tell me *nothing*. Two years after marriage, I had twin boys, the best gift any couple could ask for. I didn't know how much of a ride I would be in for. After I had the twins, I slipped into postpartum depression. I didn't want to hold my babies; it was just too much. What was I going to do with two babies? I had just finished college and had great plans, but it seemed as if they were cut off due to the circumstances of my family. My husband started working to support his family as he should. I literally never saw him, and it was draining to have the kids by myself all the time. Furthermore, my needs were not met as a wife.

We needed more money. Times were just hard. I found a job, and my husband and I flipped flopped schedules so we could meet the needs of our kids and expenses. Guess what? A trap was set, and Satan gave me just what I wanted. I met a guy who filled the voids that my husband didn't fill. He said everything I wanted him to. I didn't feel lonely anymore. I was getting the attention I craved and became prideful, nasty in my attitude, bitter, angry, and hurt. The sight of a peaceful marriage was far from us.

The arguments between my husband and I worsened, and I grew to dislike my husband. I was doing wrong, I had met someone else, which he didn't know about, and had planned to leave my husband and start a new life without him. I had no clue what I was doing and the consequences I would encounter. It blew up in my face when my husband found out what was going on. I had fallen in the trap the enemy had set up for me. I had lost focus of who I was to sexual sin and had broken my husband's heart. I thought I had dealt with this issue. He was in complete disbelief that I had done this to him. This caused so many problems that I was not prepared to face. This affair had broken me down to my core. I thought to myself, *This is it, my marriage is over. I lost my husband to fulfill the desires of my flesh.* But God touched his heart, and he forgave me. We worked on our marriage and moved on.

Things got extremely rough years later. My husband and I didn't know if we wanted to be together anymore. I felt that I got married too young and I wanted to live my life. Convenient time, right? The soul tie that I had made in my teenage years was still there. I hadn't seen this person in years. All of a sudden, he popped up out of nowhere. Again, Satan had given me exactly what I wanted. I thought I was in heaven. No, I was blind and stupid. I was

Purpose Will Prevail

dealing with sexual sin (*adultery*). *How in the world am I getting put back into the same situation?*

While I was married, I carried on a relationship with another person for years. I was hopeless, scared, and wanted out. I had abandoned many promises God had placed in my spirit. I wasn't happy, I wanted my husband, and I couldn't continue living my life like that anymore. I couldn't keep living a lie. I got on my knees and I cried out, "God, help me. I don't want to do this anymore. Change me."

I prayed and asked God to remove this deeply rooted issue of sexual sin, lust, and adultery from my heart. God radically changed my life. I didn't want my will anymore; I wanted His. Every time I would try to go back to that lifestyle, I would get so convicted in my spirit, I'd feel ridiculously uncomfortable. God totally uprooted the issue and took the taste out of my mouth. God had set me free of what held me bound for years. I have a clean conscious now. I am living the life I represent to everyone in public and in private. What a great feeling, a great place to be. I love it!

My struggle didn't start when I got married, however. My struggle started when I got exposed and brought into something caused by someone else. I allowed sin to take root in my life, and I take full responsibility for my actions. What I had experienced as a child, I acted it out. I never dealt with the issue of that situation, which caused it to grow much worse than what it was. The enemy had a plan to stop me from living in my God-given purpose from the very beginning. These plans kept me bound for years because I didn't want to fully surrender my life to God's will. My sin separated me from God. I wasn't hearing Him like I should, and things God had planted in my spirit kept dying because of my sin.

I am telling you this story to let you know I am not perfect. I was a sinner saved by grace. I will not talk to others without telling them what God delivered me from. I am not happy about my past, but guess what? It is washed in the blood of Jesus Christ. He has forgiven me. I am free. I am living my life right now as the woman God created me to be. I am walking in my purpose. I love God too much to turn back. He has done so much for me. The minute I said yes, I stepped into alignment with the will of God for my life.

When I was in sin, I wandered in circles trying to do things in my own power and it cannot be done. You may not be dealing with sexual sin, but you may be dealing with something else. Anything you stop doing only to keep returning to is an addiction, and that addiction needs to be broken off your life. Remember, sin keeps us separated from God, and if we are separated from God, how can we fulfill our purpose?

Everything I went through was unexpected, but God still had a plan. Because we live in a fallen world and are human, we will make mistakes, but we have to walk in forgiveness and grace. So whatever you are going through that is keeping you separated from God, give it up. It is not worth the heartache and pain. You have a purpose to fulfill. We cannot impact anybody's life while living a lie; we have to live in integrity. Through my process of purpose, I messed up a lot, but I am grateful I didn't stay there.

Many may be wondering what happened with my husband and I. God fully restored our marriage. We are happily married with three boys, and whenever we have problems, we talk it out without bringing up the past. God is priority in our marriage, so we walk in love and forgive. We hope to help others get through similar problems as ours. There is hope when you can't see it. I hold my head high because I am a daughter of the King. I'm going to give you some key strategies to breaking addictions over your life so that you can be set free by the power of God.

...Prayer...

Father, in the name of Jesus, I thank you that your power is greater than any addiction that tries to keep us from your presence. Father, thank you for saving us and washing us clean. Father, thank you for restoration and restored relationships from sin. Father, give us the strength to walk through any trial or temptation. Father, for those reading this book, I pray that they will have the courage to change their lifestyle and live boldly for you. Father, I come against every spirit of the enemy that will try to stop this person from walking in their purpose.

In Jesus Name,
Amen

REFLECTIONS

REFLECTIONS

6

Deliverance: Breaking the Power of Addiction

Addiction is characterized by the inability to consistently abstain, impairment in behavioral control, cravings, diminished recognition of significant problems with one's behaviors and interpersonal relationships, and a dysfunctional emotional response. Like other chronic diseases, addiction often involves cycles of relapse and remission. Without treatment or engagement in recovery activities, addiction is progressive and can result in disability or premature death.

~American Society of Addiction Medicine

Being addicted to something or someone is powerful. When something is too strong for you to handle, and you consistently do it—even though you know it is wrong and will hurt the people around you, including God—you are addicted. You want to stop, but you can't because your flesh needs this addiction to survive. You think you need this addiction to survive or live a great life. It makes your flesh feel good. While still in my sin, I needed a way out from my addiction. It needed to be broken, and God taught me how to break this bondage of addiction and stay free. God is a wonderful counselor. Nothing can be broken and uprooted without the power of God. Galatians 5:19-21 gives a list of sins that need to be broken off our lives, and addictions is one.

It is obvious what kind of life develops out of trying to get your own way all the time: repetitive, loveless, cheap sex; a stinking accumulation of mental and emotional garbage; frenzied and joyless grabs for happiness; trinket gods; magic-show religion; paranoid loneliness; cutthroat competition; all-consuming-yet-never-satisfied wants; a brutal temper; an impotence to love or be loved; divided homes and divided lives; small-minded and lopsided pursuits; the vicious habit of depersonalizing everyone into a rival; uncontrolled and uncontrollable addictions; ugly parodies of community. I could go on. This isn't the first time I have warned you, you know. If you use your freedom this way, you will not inherit God's kingdom (The Message Bible).

I don't know about you, but I wanted to be freed from my addiction. Today, if you want to be free, you can break any addiction that has you in bondage. Don't live another day bound when you have the power to be set free from anything holding you captive. You have a purpose to be fulfilled, and you cannot accomplish it while held hostage by sin. Let's break these addictions, especially curses that go from generation to generation. There are many families dealing with addictions, wondering why they are dealing with certain things. It is because the sin was never dealt with. Instead, it was passed down. Let's deal with it today.

I have four profound, yet simple principles that will lead you into deliverance and keep you delivered. Nothing is done overnight, so don't get discouraged. Continue actively putting these four principles into action:

- Confront it.
- Confess it.
- Expose it.
- Denounce it.

Therefore confess your sins to each other and pray for each other so that you may be healed. The prayer of a righteous person is powerful and effective (James 5:16, NIV).

••• *Principle #1: Confront it*

It is time to come face to face with the issues and sins that have been holding you in bondage for so long, keeping you from your purpose. Let's talk about why you are dealing with the issue or sin. Get in the face of sin and confront it. Get to the deep root of the issue. *Why am I doing this?* Talk it out with God. Ask Him to reveal it to you.

••• *Principle #2: Confess it*

When we confess, we admit and acknowledge that we are doing wrong. We acknowledge the fact that we have sinned before God and we want forgiveness. We realize we have a problem and it needs to be fixed. Right now, I want you to confess that problem, sin, addiction, or disobedience you have been dealing with. Talk it out with God.

Purpose Will Prevail

> ### ••• *Principle #3: Expose it*
>
> We have to tell someone trustworthy about the issue or sin. We have to uncover the sin. Most of the time when we are doing wrong, we like to hide behind the sin and commit it behind closed doors. If you are willing to expose it, and have someone hold you accountable, you will see the difference in you wanting to commit that sin. Find an accountability partner. Talk it out together, and talk it out with God.
>
> ### ••• *Principle #4: Denounce it*
>
> We have to denounce that issue or sin that is trying to hold us captive. Reject it when it comes knocking, and do not open the door. Let the knocking keep going. After a while, it will stop. Betray it, so it will leave you alone. Publicly declare it as wrong, and let the issue or sin know that it will not control your life anymore because it is not welcome. Disown it. Talk it out with God.

These principles are powerful because they deal with what we speak. *The tongue has the power of life and death, and those who love it will eat its fruit (Proverbs 18:21, NIV).*

What we speak has power. Our tongue can produce life or death, and we will reap the benefit or destruction of it. So if we make a daily habit of confronting, confessing, exposing, and denouncing our sin, we will see the fruit of what we have been speaking, and the fruit of us speaking life will break that bondage and lead to deliverance. Silent people stay captive because they do not have the weapons of warfare in their mouth to get free. The main reason I was bound for so long was because I stopped praying; the enemy muted my mouth. I was so deep in sin I was ashamed to go to God. Let me tell you, the minute you open your mouth, deliverance is on the way.

When you begin to speak life and accept the forgiveness of the Lord, you will begin to see the fruit of your labor. When you are free of sin, you will experience a great amount of joy and freedom. The feeling of being condemned or ashamed will leave because it can't stay where it is not welcomed. It is powerful how circumstances in our life change due to the power of our words. The fruit of speaking life is living a life of purpose.

You have power, and if you ever find out the kind of power you hold, you will turn this world upside down. Satan knows how powerful you are, and when you find out who you are, he is in trouble. We cannot help people while still bound ourselves. That just causes an increase of chaos. The most powerful thing is to get free because once a bound person is free, they have the ability to liberate others. Once you're freed, watch that dream and purpose that was dormant come alive.

Once you are loosed from captivity, a sense of power and authority is restored back to you. There will always be temptation because we are human, but you have to protect yourself and your purpose as you continue on the journey. Walking with God is not easy, but He has equipped us with the power, tools, and strategies to be able to walk in our purpose with confidence. You have all power over the enemy. Resist him, and he will flee.

... _Prayer_ ...

Father, in the name of Jesus, I thank you today that every chain is broken, every sin and addiction that is keeping this reader from their purpose will be broken. Father, I come against every generational curse, that the curse will be broken and uprooted. I loose the blood of Jesus to cover minds that have been released from captivity. Father, for those who need clarity on issues, reveal it to them, so that they may be set free.

In Jesus Name,
Amen

REFLECTIONS

REFLECTIONS

7

Breaking the Spirit of Fear

The negative kind of fear rips, tears, paralyzes, and torments. It destroys our faith in God and His Word and opens us up to further harassment of the devil. Negative fear is a satanic region.

-Kimberly Daniels

Fear will take away your faith and hold you hostage from your purpose and the promises God has for your life. My fear was mainly a spiritual battle; it was the worst fear I have had to swallow. Everything I speak of is real. I know what fear looks like, smells like, and feels like. I felt like fear had gripped itself around my neck and sucked the life out of me. Fear looks different for everyone, and the fear I experienced tried to keep me from my purpose.

According to Dictionary.Reference.com, fear is caused by a threat that is either real or imagined. Examples of fears that we face are of:

- Commitment
- Being alone

- Darkness
- Public speaking
- The unknown
- Water
- Taking risks
- Death
- Intimacy
- Rejection
- Failure
- Success

Individuals with these fears have their valid reason of why they are afraid, when it comes to these things. There is a difference between understanding that fear exists and that we may experience it, and living a fearful life. Even though the environments around us produce fear, we have to learn to overcome it by learning the root cause of it and by standing on the word of God and what He says about fear. We must also walk in the authority He has given us to overcome fear. This is with any type of fear because what may seem small to one person may be a big deal for others. There are different levels of fear. Let's look at some scriptures concerning fear;

- *There is no fear in love; but perfect love casts out fear, because fear involves torment. But he who fears has not been made perfect in love (1 John 4:8, NKJV).*

- *Whenever I am afraid, I will trust in You (Psalm 56:3, NKJV).*

- *In God (I will praise His word), In God I have put my trust; I will not fear. What can flesh do to me. (Psalm 56:4, NKJV)*

- *Do not be afraid of their faces, For I am with you to deliver you," says the LORD. (Jeremiah 1:8, NKJV)*

- *Overhearing what they said, Jesus told him, "Don't be afraid; just believe." (Mark 5:36, NIV)*

- *The fear of man brings a snare, But whoever trusts in the LORD shall be safe. (Proverbs 29:25, NKJV)*

- *Say to those who are fearful-hearted, "Be strong, do not fear! Behold, your God will come with vengeance, with the recompense of God; He will come and save you. (Isaiah 35:4 (NKJV)*

- *Do not fear, for you will not be ashamed; Neither be disgraced, for you will not be put to shame; For you will forget the shame of your youth, And will not remember the reproach of your widowhood anymore. (Isaiah 54:4, NKJV)*

- *For the Lord your God is living among you. He is a mighty savior. He will take delight in you with gladness. With his love, he will calm all your fears. He will rejoice over you with joyful songs. (Zephaniah 3:17, NLT)*

Purpose Will Prevail

- *We faced conflict from every direction, with battles on the outside and fear on the inside. But God, who encourages those who are discouraged, encouraged us by the arrival of Titus. His presence was a joy. (2 Corinthians 7:5-6, NLT)*

- *Even though I walk through the darkest valley, I will fear no evil, for you are with me. (Psalm 23:4, NIV)*

- *Do not be afraid of anyone, for judgment belongs to God. (Deuteronomy 1:17, NIV)*

- *Do not be afraid of them; the LORD your God himself will fight for you. (Deuteronomy, 3:22 NIV)*

- *The LORD is my light and my salvation— whom shall I fear? The LORD is the stronghold of my life— of whom shall I be afraid? (Psalm 27:1, NIV)*

- *He said to his disciples, "Why are you so afraid? Do you still have no faith?" (Mark 4:40 NIV)*

- *Then he placed his right hand on me and said: "Do not be afraid. I am the First and the Last. (Revelation 1:17, NIV)*

I have given you many verses to meditate on what God says concerning fear. The anxiety we have, we are supposed to give to God. If you become fearful about anything, it should only be for a moment because, at that point, you have to recognize who you are and whose you are. Because God is concerned about every detail of our life. If you read each scripture, you will notice that every circumstance was different, but through the midst of it all, He wants us to trust Him. While walking in purpose, fear will arise. I'm talking about the fear that brings you to a halt in fulfilling your calling; that spirit needs to be broken.

Be strong and of good courage, do not fear nor be afraid of them; for the LORD your God, He is the One who goes with you. He will not leave you nor forsake you (Deuteronomy 31:6, NKJV)

After accepting Jesus Christ as my Lord and Savior, one of the greatest decisions I had made, my life had completely been turned upside down. All I wanted to do was spend time with God and get to know who He was. His word was literally my daily food. I didn't know much about the spiritual side of things, or about Satan, but I was about to find out. Experiencing these spiritual attacks was terrifying, but it birthed a great power and authority in me that needed to be released. Satan doesn't like us living out the will of God for our lives, so he sends fiery darts to try to stop us in any way he can. Whatever your purpose is connected to, believe me when I say there will be a fight because our purpose is connected to the creator. The enemy's goal is to keep us separated from God.

I experienced one of my first spiritual attacks while sleeping. The first time it happened, I fell asleep and I woke up with a fear that paralyzed me from the head down. It was as if a spirit held me down so I couldn't move. I tried with everything in me to speak and move, but I had no victory. After this night, fear had attached itself to me, and I was afraid to go to sleep. I would stay up all night or sleep with my parents because I didn't want to experience this type of fear again. The anxiety was so heavy, I would be tired, but I couldn't go to sleep. If I closed my eyes, I would wake up quickly. Every time I fell asleep, I would experience the same attack. I was devastated and confused as to why this was happening to me. Because of my reaction, Satan knew that this one particular thing could keep me in fear if I continued to accept it, or didn't respond with authority.

What I am describing to you, some people will call sleep paralysis; it features waking up from sleep and being temporarily unable to move. It is often accompanied by visual hallucinations and fear (Mellman et al., 2008). It is an action or strategy carefully planned to achieve a specific end. It is a tactic of the enemy to plant fear and confusion in our hearts. Treatment plans consist of making sure you get enough sleep or using an antidepressant to help regulate sleep, but the method I used to become free worked, and I have never had to fight this spiritual battle again. I call it a spiritual battle because it was unseen of what was happening to me with the natural eye, and I needed God's help in pinpointing what was tormenting me. Even God has given us the power to cast sickness from our bodies with His power. *And when He had called His twelve disciples to Him, He gave them power over unclean spirits, to cast them out, and to heal all kinds of sickness and all kinds of disease (Matthew 10:1, NKJV).* Whether you say it was demons or sleep paralysis, it had to go. *Lest Satan should take advantage of us; for we are not ignorant of his devices (2 Corinthians 2:11, NKJV).* I do not accept everything for what people say it is. I go to God about it, and let Him reveal it to me. If I would have accepted that I had sleep paralysis, if that's what it was, I would still be dealing with it today, trying to treat it man's way and not God's.

Can you imagine waking up every night tormented by spirits, and not knowing why this is happening to you, or how to get out? I was so freaked out. My back had to be against a wall while sitting in a room because I could feel the presence of something evil. As I continued to read the Bible and pray, it was as if God was showing me how to break free of fear. I began to practice my authority, and it changed my life. God sometimes allows us to go through certain situations in life to teach us and show us that everything we need is inside of us. I learned that I was not practicing the tools given to me to overcome the enemy.

Standing in the bathroom, I remember looking in the mirror. I turned my head and saw a spirit of a demon that looked like an old lady. Again, fear had risen up in my heart. It terrified me. What was going on, why was I seeing this, and experiencing all of this demonic activity? When I started experiencing moments like this, fear would captivate my mind, and I would keep replaying the experiences in my head. I would pray, but I wouldn't really release my power to get physically and mentally free.

I was at a friend's house who I'd always hung out with. Nothing could separate us, but this one incident kept me from going to her house for months. I was lying on the bed on my back, and my eyes opened quickly because I was straddled by what I had heard. When I opened my eyes, I heard the (audible) voice of Satan. The voice was evil, so I knew it wasn't God, and there was no peace in it at all. What the enemy did was keep me bound in fear by making me think it was the house. I did not want to go back to my friend's house, period. Every time she asked, I made up an excuse as to why I couldn't come over. The enemy tried to keep me in fear and away from anything or anyone that would keep me close to God.

By now, I'm thinking, *Okay, Jasma. You're missing something here. Why does this keep happening to you?* Then I remembered that greater is He, that is in me, that is in the world. I began activating the power that was inside of me. This is when I truly learned how to pray! In high school, I had experiences and overcame them little by little, but one day I couldn't take the torment anymore. I was in college, in my dorm room, and this spirit of fear was still attached to me because I had not broken it off my life. As I lay down to go to bed, it happened again. I was being paralyzed, unable to move, fighting to get free. Authority hit my spirit, and I began to speak the blood of Jesus in my head and it came out my mouth. As I repeated, "*The blood of Jesus, Jesus, Jesus, Jesus*," I begin to pray, and I was extremely mad too. I prayed with authority, and declared, "No more! This ends right now! Leave me alone!" The spirit of fear ceased. It left me and has not returned.

Overcoming the spirit of fear was a challenge, but with the help of God, I was able to break that spirit off of my life. Prayer, the Bible, the blood of Jesus, and faith played a major role in breaking this spirit. Putting these four action-based principles together defeated the spirit of fear that was attached to my life. My faith gave me the confidence to pray what the Holy Spirit put in my spirit. Through prayer, I bonded and loosed the spirits of the enemy that came to cause confusion. Praying the blood of Jesus allowed me to cover myself and speak against every evil spirit because evil spirits cannot cross the blood of Jesus. The blood of Jesus is a protective coating that keeps us from hurt, harm, and danger. Faith allowed me to believe what I was saying, and I watched the principles work just like the Bible spoke of them to do.

I now live my life free of fear from natural and spiritual things. Once I had come to the knowledge of who God was and who I was, that was it! I had a right to be free from anything that held me captive. When you realize who you are, the enemy is afraid of what you can do because when you start to fully operate in who you are, the enemy has no authority. Fear may look different in your life, however. What is it that you fear and need broken off your life? Do not live your life in fear. Live your life in purpose. Through the pain and pressure of fear, I experienced authority and dominion, and a prayer warrior was birthed. I understood the battle and the fight of dealing with fear when I saw what I gained. Warring in the spirit is important when detaching spirits from your life. They don't leave easily, but you have the authority to make them go. When I began to pray, I was amazed at what was coming out of me. When I prayed, things would break, and the presence of God showed up mightily. I wanted to deal with two types of fears that I believe are important in walking in your assignment: general fears and fears that bring

Purpose Will Prevail

torment. Again, they are present in this world, but we don't have to be fearful when walking with God.

The only person I fear is God, and that is a holy fear. It is reverence that I hold toward God. It is not a fear that keeps me bound, but one that sets me free. I fear for people who do not know God. People who don't know Jesus and live their life without him is a burden that I carry. It ties a knot in my heart knowing that people die and leave this earth not knowing Jesus. My passion is to share the gospel and bring people to the Savior, Jesus Christ. When I tell you my story of fear, it is not to scare you, but to let you know that if I didn't have Jesus in my life and the revelation of how to overcome and break that spirit of fear and other spirits, I can guarantee I would have been labeled as crazy or abnormal. *The Bible states in Ephesians 6:12, For our struggle is not against flesh and blood, but against the rulers, against the authorities, against the powers of this dark world and against the spiritual forces of evil in the heavenly realms (NIV).*

We are afraid of the unknown, but we don't have to be. God is on our side. God is a God that never sleeps; He looks out for us 24/7. I don't know about you, but I am glad I have a God that cares about me deeply and will never leave nor forsake me.

The LORD himself goes before you and will be with you; he will never leave you nor forsake you. Do not be afraid; do not be discouraged (Deuteronomy 31:8, NIV).

Let's walk through this together and break that spirit of fear today, so that you can walk in purpose with confidence, dominion and authority.

Grab your journal or a piece of paper, and a pen, and write your responses to the following questions:

- What fear has attached itself to your life?

- Do you fear dying? Do you fear being alone? Do you have spiritual attacks that you can't explain? Do you fear your past? Do you fear the lack there of? Do you fear people? Do you fear what lies ahead? Do you fear how big your purpose is?

It's okay! Today, it stops. Let's move forward. Let's get active. You have to do the work to be set free.

Talk it out with God:

What have you been fearful of? What is stopping you from walking in your purpose?

Now every word you just spoke to God, He heard and is waiting to move on your behalf. One of the worst things you can do when breaking a stronghold off your life is to remain silent. When we remain silent, we allow the enemy to bully us and keep us in bondage. There is help and a way out!

Purpose Will Prevail

Let's pray. Say it with me:

Father, in the name of Jesus, we come against the spirit of fear. We break the root of fear, and command it to leave our lives, homes, and minds. Fear, you have no place in our life. Your assignment for our life has been officially canceled. We bind you in the name of Jesus. Loosen your hold *now*! We plead the blood of Jesus over our bodies and mind! We send angels on assignment to make every crooked place straight. Father, we thank you that we are free and able to walk in full confidence to fulfill our purpose.

In Jesus Name,
Amen

Now pray your prayer of faith in your own words:

••• *Thankfulness*

- Father, thank you for freedom today. Thanks for setting us free from the spirit of fear. Now we can boldly walk in our purpose that was created for us.

- Father, thank you for equipping us for purpose.

- Father, thank you for loving us unconditionally.

- Father, thank you for never leaving us nor forsaking us.

- Father, thank you for joy.

- Father, thank you for confidence, dominion, and authority.

- Father, thank you for peace.

- Father, thank you for keeping us when we experience the unknown.

`If the spirit of fear is not broken, you cannot and will not walk in the purpose God has designed for your life. Fear comes to paralyze and choke the life out of us. When we live in fear, we are letting the plan of Satan prevail over God's plan. If you choose fear over freedom, power, and authority, expect to live an unfulfilled life. Fear will have you answer to man, and not God. God has the power to make every spirit bow at His knee, and so do you.

For God has not given us a spirit of fear, but of power and of love and of a sound mind (2 Timothy 1:7, NKJV).

Purpose Will Prevail

... Prayer ...

Father, in the name of Jesus, we thank you for giving us the power and the authority to be able to cast down the spirit of fear and walk in confidence. Father, thank you for removing the scales from our eyes that we may see clearly and be aware of the devices of the enemy. Father, we thank you that the enemy is defeated and that his plans are null and void. Father we loose the blood of Jesus to cover and protect us from the crown of our head to the soles of our feet. Father, we thank you for peace that surpasses all understanding, and we take joy in knowing that you are our protector.

In Jesus Name,
Amen

REFLECTIONS

REFLECTIONS

8

Protecting Your Purpose

And we know that for those who love God all things work together for good, for those who are called according to his purpose

(Romans 8:28, NKJV).

It is highly imperative that you protect the calling that was designed for you before the foundation of the world. We understand that we have a purpose and that we were created to release that purpose into the earth. Through years of understanding purpose, I have found out how vital it is to protect it. There have been many ideas that God has impregnated me with that I have aborted by my own lack of understanding. I hadn't disciplined myself to use the principles laid out for me in the word of God. Though simple, these principles take discipline to maintain. Otherwise, you'll continually fall into sin over and over again. Let's take a look at some principles and strategies that will lead us into successfully fulfilling our purpose.

Purpose Will Prevail

••• *What is your purpose?*

In order to protect your purpose, you must know what it is. To discover your purpose, you have to pursue Christ relentlessly. You have to seek God, faithfully, never slacking in your search. The Bible tells us in Jeremiah 29:13, *And you will seek Me and find Me, when you search for Me with all your heart.* We never find out what our calling is because we stop seeking God. When we seek God, He will make himself known to us, and everything else will follow. *But seek first the kingdom of God and His righteousness, and all these things shall be added to you* (Matthew 6:33, NKJV).

We have to know and understand the voice of God because the more we seek God and spend time with Him, we begin to understand His voice, and how He speaks to us. When you know the voice of God, it's easier to follow Him and go forth in what you are called to do. *My sheep hear My voice, and I know them, and they follow Me (John 10:27, NKJV).* The more you spend time with God, the more you begin to take on His characteristics, and the more you become like God, the more you will begin to walk in your calling.

After seeking God and knowing His voice, God will begin to reveal your purpose. God doesn't just drop a boatload of stuff on you. He shows you in part by giving you ideas, dreams, and visions. If God showed us everything at once, we wouldn't complete the tasks. Because what God has for us is beyond what we can do in the natural; we need His assistance. He is the potter, and we are the clay. He has to shape and equip us as we go along the way. God will drop little nuggets in your spirit about your assignment that will amaze you, but it drives you to pursue your purpose.

Studying God's Word is very important because it is our instruction manual to living our godly life. God also speaks to us through his Word. *All Scripture is God-breathed and is useful for teaching, rebuking, correcting and training in righteousness* (2 Timothy 3:16, NIV). It is when we study God's Word that it gets in our hearts, and when it gets in our hearts, we begin to live by His word and perform it. The Bible is still relevant to our situations and circumstances today and always provides God's best for His children. *Do your best to present yourself to God as one approved, a worker who does not need to be ashamed and who correctly handles the word of truth* (2 Thimothy 2:15, NIV). As my Pastor would say, pursuing God's best will help you find your purpose.

After God speaks to you about your purpose, He will strategically place people in your life who are connected to your purpose and will confirm the words He has spoken to you. Some will help you for a season, and some will help you for a lifetime. These people will be likeminded and imitators of Christ. It will amaze you how detailed God is when He places certain people in your life. God will always send help. *I will lift up my eyes to the hills—from whence comes my help? My help comes from the LORD, Who made heaven and earth* (Psalm 121: 1-2, NKJV).

Imagine the outline of a tree. It has a trunk that is rooted in the ground, and out of that trunk grows stems and

Purpose Will Prevail

leaves. Without the trunk of the tree, how can the leaves stand? Your purpose is that deeply rooted trunk, representing that deeply rooted passion in your heart that is too big for the natural mind to comprehend. Out of that passion, many things pertaining to your purpose will grow. Without purpose, these things could not stand.

For an example, let's say your purpose was to be a messenger. That is the root, the trunk of the tree. Now it's time to get that message out to the world. So you have creative ideas to get your message out. You write a book, birth a radio show, then develop products and programs to further deliver that message. Your ultimate purpose never changes, but you birth several babies and ideas like the leaves on the tree to fulfill your purpose. **What is your PURPOSE?**

••• *Accepting your purpose!*

Once God has revealed your purpose to you, the choice is yours to whether you accept the call or not. I love the fact that God gives us free will to choose. Yes, you have a choice whether or not to accept the purpose God has planned for your life. I can tell you, it won't be the best plan if you don't accept. Accepting your God-given purpose lets God know that you agree with His plan for your life. Remember that fear is not an option. Even though we don't know the exact detailed plan, God does. Trust me, it will be okay. *Trust in the LORD with all your heart and lean not on your own understanding; in all your ways submit to him, and he will make your paths straight (Proverbs 3:5-6, NIV).* **Will you accept your PURPOSE?**

••• *Understanding and listening to the voice of God!*

God talks to His people. He is always speaking, and it is important that we align ourselves in a position that we can always hear God. Oftentimes we are so busy moving, we never take the time out to sit and communicate with God. What does God's voice sound like? It is different for every person; God speaks to people on their level so they'll understand when God communicates to them. It's that still small voice that speaks to your heart. God sometimes speaks in an audible voice, as well as through dreams and visions. I guarantee you, as your relationship with Christ grows, you will know the voice of God. *My sheep listen to my voice; I know them, and they follow me (John 10:27, NIV).* **Is God SPEAKING to you?**

••• *Prayer!*

Prayer is one of the most powerful, effective tools in living an action filled, purpose-driven life. Without prayer, there is no way one could live out their purpose. Prayer has got me through some rough times and has empowered me to stand. There would be times I didn't pray, and it changed everything. I saw a difference in my walk with God. I wasn't as focused and became double-minded in my ways. I was confused about everything and really didn't like being in that place. Prayer keeps me humbled and in consistent communication with God. What you speak out of your mouth protects the purpose you carry. There is power of life and death in the tongue: You can give life to your purpose or abort it. *The prayer of a righteous person is powerful and effective (James 5:16, NIV).* **Are you PRAYING?**

••• *Fasting!*

Fasting is an important principle to practice as it will keep you on track and balanced. Fasting is the abstinence from food or drink, or both. Fasting is to turn down something of normal intake and is important when walking in purpose. It clears your mind and cuts off the things that are not of God. When fasting, prayer has to be combined to be fully effective. I have been fasting for years, and the reward of fasting will truly change your life. I remember completing a three day water fast with no food and was able to think and meditate on the things of God much more clearly. I heard God and the things He was speaking into my life. I had dreams like crazy, and revelation was given to me about my purpose. The combination of prayer, fasting, and reading your Bible is one of the most effective ways of protecting your purpose. If you have health issues, please talk to the appropriate professional before you fast. **Are you FASTING?**

••• *Reading your Bible!*

God's Word is our instruction on how to live an abundant life according to our purpose. Reading the Bible is another way to practice understanding the voice of God and what He is saying for your life and your purpose for your life. It keeps us in line with our purpose and teaches us how to pray, what to pray, when to speak, and when to be silent. We have to make the word active in our life so it works for us in every area. The Bible also teaches us how to fight against the enemy and to be aware of his schemes. The enemy has no new schemes. The same nonsense he tried on Jesus, he tries on us every day, but Jesus overcame it by the Word of God. *All Scripture is given by inspiration of God, and is profitable for doctrine, for reproof, for correction, for instruction in righteousness (2 Timothy 3:16, NKJV).* **Are you reading the BIBLE?**

••• *Spiritual Warfare!*

There will be times when you will have to be in war with the enemy to protect your purpose, but that is okay. The Bible gives us principles on taking authority and defeating Satan. It is important that we are always ready to put Satan in his place. Let's look at Ephesians 6: 10-20: *Finally, my brethren, be strong in the Lord and in the power of His might. Put on the whole armor of God, that you may be able to stand against the wiles of the devil. For we do not wrestle against flesh and blood, but against principalities, against powers, against the rulers of the darkness of this age, against spiritual hosts of wickedness in the heavenly places. Therefore take up the whole armor of God, that you may be able to withstand in the evil day, and having done all, to stand.*

Stand therefore, having girded your waist with truth, having put on the breastplate of righteousness, and having shod your feet with the preparation of the gospel of peace; above all, taking the shield of faith with which you will be able to quench all the fiery darts of the wicked one. And take the helmet of salvation, and the sword of the Spirit, which is the word of God; praying always with all

Purpose Will Prevail

prayer and supplication in the Spirit, being watchful to this end with all perseverance and supplication for all the saints and for me, that utterance may be given to me, that I may open my mouth boldly to make known the mystery of the gospel, for which I am an ambassador in chains; that in it I may speak boldly, as I ought to speak (NKJV).

Putting on the full armor of God is what we need to protect our purpose; the full armor of God keeps us equipped and ready for anything. The Lord will fight all of our battles because we are His children. The full armor of God is the belt of truth buckled around your waist, the breastplate of righteousness, gospel of peace, shield of faith, helmet of salvation, and the sword of the Spirit, which is the word of God. We are to pray daily, without ceasing, and on all occasions, prayer helps us stay equipped and ready for battle. As we go from day to day, we must make sure that we fully put on the armor of God, and operate in it. **Do you have the armor of God on?**

••• *Declaration!*

Declaration is powerful. It is joined with faith, and both are needed in the process of purpose because we have to be able to declare things before we see it. Job 22:28 states, *You will also declare a thing, And it will be established for you; So light will shine on your ways (NKJV).* In walking with God, we have to have faith. Without faith, it is impossible to please God. Faith allows us to declare and command what God said will be. We have to declare even when situations don't look good. After all, it is by faith that we believe and know that God is working on our behalf.

Declare daily that it will happen, whatever it is, according to the will of God. **Are you declaring that your purpose come to pass?**

••• *Resources!*

Gather resources pertaining to your purpose and become the expert on what you were created to do. Resources can also mean people. Who are you supposed to be connected to? We cannot fulfill purpose alone. We need people and divine connections. Do not steal the ideas of others, but rather gather your own resources to become knowledgeable of the things that were done already. Your purpose is unique and catered to who you are. Your purpose is always to serve others. How are you supposed to serve others around you with your purpose? If you are developing an online course, gather resources on how to develop online courses. *Hosea 4:6, states that we are destroyed from lack of knowledge (NIV).* Seek resources that line up with the Word of God to help you fulfill your purpose. **What RESOURCES do you have?**

••• *The Blood of Jesus!*

Oh, the blood of Jesus. The blood of Jesus has gotten me through some rough times. The blood is powerful and always working on our behalf. Speak the blood daily for protection of self and purpose. The blood is a protector, a covering for God's people. It is so important that we are using and releasing the blood of Christ in our everyday life. Because of the world that we live in, there should not be a day that goes by that we do not effectively speak and release the blood of Jesus Christ. It confirms our covenant with God. The enemy desires to take us out, stop us, and distract us so that we will not enter into covenant with Christ because he knows the significance of the blood and how powerful it is when we use it. Proclaiming and declaring the blood will help you establish authority and dominion in the earth. Without the blood of the Lamb, we would live in a world without Jesus and without hope. *And according to the law almost all things are purified with blood, and without shedding of blood there is no remission (Hebrews 9:22, NKJV).* When we stop speaking and pleading the blood, we stop speaking life. Release the blood in both your prayer and declarations daily. We are safe under the blood. Demons may not cross over it. God will defend and protect us according to the blood because it's a binding agreement made with our covenant. Why is the blood so important? It is LIFE! *"The life of a creation is in his blood" (Leviticus, 17:11, NIV).* Activate the blood of Christ in your life. Pray for the unbelievers, and do not start your day without putting on your coat (the blood). Speak the blood of Jesus over your purpose in order to cover and protect it. **Are you pleading the BLOOD?**

••• *Praise and Worship!*

We were all created to worship God. When walking in purpose, it gets tough and the pressure can seem to be too much, but when we praise God, He shows up, and you will be surprised how quickly the pressure or burden is lifted. God gives a garment of praise for the spirit of heaviness.

To console those who mourn in Zion, To give them beauty for ashes, The oil of joy for mourning, The garment of praise for the spirit of heaviness; That they may be called trees of righteousness, The planting of the LORD, *that He may be glorified (Is. 61:3, NKJV).*

Praise protects your purpose by helping you get through difficult times; it gets you past what situations look like, so you can focus on the nature of God instead.

Worship is important because it is intimate; it is into God you see. When we worship God, nothing else matters. Often times, I just sit in God's presence. Worship is an awe moment, a breath-taking experience, where no one else gets the glory but God. When we worship God, we see who we really are. Only the truth can live in the presence of God, and He is seeking true worshippers. *God is Spirit, and those who worship Him must worship in spirit and truth (John 4:24, NKJV).*

Everything mentioned in this chapter is crucial to protecting your purpose. It is important that we understand and use the principles God has expressed in His Word. God has given you everything you need to fulfill your purpose. Don't be hesitant to step into it. I have come to realize that what God has placed inside me is beyond my capability to fulfill, so I have to trust God with everything. And if I can be honest, trusting God is not easy through hard times, but it is through the hard times that we learn to trust. Moments of pressure produced faith and increased my trust and dependency on God. As much as we should learn to protect our purpose, we must trust God with it.

Purpose Will Prevail

... Prayer ...

Father, in the name of Jesus, teach us how to protect our purpose. Help us to use the strategies and principles in your Word. Let us speak life to our purpose versus negative words. Father, we thank you for divine revelation and insight on how to impact the world with what you have placed inside of us. Father, teach us to pray your Word over our life in faith. Father, we release the blood of Jesus to cover and protect us through the process of purpose. Father, teach us your voice as we communicate with you daily.

In Jesus Name,
Amen

REFLECTIONS

REFLECTIONS

9

Trust God with Your Purpose

Every word of God is pure;
He is a shield to those who put their trust in Him

(Proverbs 30:5, NKJV).

When we purchase a product from the store that needs to be assembled, directions come with the package on how to put the product together. The store you purchased the product from did not give you directions; the manufacturer did. You trust, without even second guessing sometimes, that the creator of the product knows what he is doing because he created it. When the product malfunctions, we do not go to the manufacturer, we go to the store to either see what's wrong or to get a new product. In this process, we never really know what the root of the problem is because it is a quick fix, but if we went back to the creator of the product, he would be able to tell us what exactly is wrong and how to fix it.

This analogy is similar to how we treat God when it comes to purpose. The creator of the universe, our Father, created us for a purpose, and when we were born, we came with instructions on how to live our lives. We were created

Purpose Will Prevail

with everything we need to fulfill our purpose. After finding out what our purpose is, we must trust God with it. We must trust and believe that He knows best. When something malfunctions in our life, we think that God lost control, when He is actually always in control; we just don't like dealing with pressure. Like the product from the store, we go to the middleman and tell them our problems; we go to people who have no idea about purpose or what to do with it. We are looking for a quick fix, or a short-term solution, to make us feel better. We have to go back to the creator, the one who has all the answers, despite what it looks like. We have to stop looking for answers outside of the source.

God is all knowing and powerful. He is able to get to the root of the issue, and give you long-term answers on how to fix it for real, for real. We continue to walk around confused and unfulfilled because we are not trusting God with our purpose. We have to surrender our will, and pick up the will of God for our lives. Trust is mutual in a relationship with God. We need to be able to trust God, and God needs to be able to trust us with what He has placed inside of us. You are a powerful spiritual being with purpose. Know who you are to walk in your purpose. *Trust in the LORD with all your heart and lean not on your own understanding; in all your ways submit to him, and he will make your paths straight (Proverbs 3:5-6, NIV).*

Before I got married, my husband asked me, "If God told me to pick up my family and go live in another city, would you trust me and go?" My response was of course, why not. I trusted him and the God in him. Little did I know, this statement would come to pass in 2011. My husband heard God say go, and I asked where. He said we are to go to St. Louis to help a certain couple build a church. My response went from *sure* to what, why, and who? Isn't it amazing how we speak things, but when it's time to take action, we forget what we said before? I was comfortable with my life and job. Everything was good, but there was one thing, I had gotten too comfortable with life and too comfortable with God. It was like I said I have a purpose, but I am going to do it my way, knowing that would only last for a short period of time. After my husband shared this information with me, I became really defensive and unwilling to follow him all of a sudden.

I was afraid of leaving what I had known for years for something new. As a result, I turned into a completely different person and was very hard to deal with. There was no convincing me that God said anything. I had let fear convince me that my husband was wrong, but deep down in my heart, I knew that something was right. My husband hears God clearly, and that had not changed the day he told me it was time to go. Even though I was fearful, I still had a reverence and respect for God not to be foolish. God spoke to me and said that He was taking me from a place of comfort to purpose.

Comfort is a purpose killer. Little did I know, I was about to enter the most uncomfortable season of my life. My husband and I picked up everything and left Omaha, first stopping in Chicago for a year to with live with my mother while we worked and saved money. The process was uncomfortable and long, but it needed to be done. We

Purpose Will Prevail

both needed to be healed of some things before we could serve this couple.

The enemy had traps set up like no other, but God was faithful and still is. We got to Chicago and my husband worked two jobs to save money for our departure from Chicago. The process in Chicago was painful and the pressure was heavy, but God got ahold of me and changed my life once again. My husband carried me in the spirit for a while because my faith was weak, but I got to a place where I knew the only person I could go to was God, my creator. I needed Him; I needed to spend some serious time with Him. Every time I tried to do something out of the will of God, I was convicted so bad I couldn't sit still. Something was stirring in my belly. It was like God was saying, "It is time to walk in your purpose." See, God had to take me away from what was comfortable and familiar to me to get me to a place where He had my attention. He sure got it, and I am grateful that God knows me better than I know myself.

There were many times my husband and I struggled because of what it looked like naturally, but God was teaching us to trust Him in spite of. I contemplated going back to Omaha many times, but God would not let me. Repeatedly, I was told to trust Him. My husband had a vision that spoke to my heart, and I know that we made the right decision to leave our comfortable place. The vision went like this: He was standing in the living room and felt an uneasy presence in the room, so he stood up. Three black dogs entered the living room from the front door and circled him multiple times. Then a white dog walked down the stairs from the room we slept in and stood next to my husband while the dogs circled him. There was one black dog that was slightly bigger than the rest, whom my husband assumed was the leader. The dog said, "You are not going to make it here; it's only going to get worse. You need to take your ass back to Omaha." The dogs began to growl and bark, and then they left out the front door. The white dog went back upstairs to sit at the foot of the bed.

My husband told me the vision the next morning, and it sent chills down my spine. I knew this battle was real, but the white dog represented our protection. The enemy tried to scare us by throwing threats, but we knew that the Lord was with us. After this vision was revealed to me, I fought harder because I knew that something great was in the works for us. We were in a season of preparation for the move to St. Louis. A year later, we moved to St. Louis and everything seemed to be going well. We had everything we needed, but that soon would change. My husband was the only one working. He supported the family financially, and I stayed home and took care of the kids. I told myself this truly was the time to get to know God; it was just me and Him.

We had come to a hard place in our lives and were trying to figure out how we had gotten there. We got to a place where we had absolutely nothing. We didn't know how we were going to make it. I have three boys, so they were my main concern. I didn't know how my kids would eat, I didn't know how we would get gas or wash clothes, but can I tell you that my God is a provider. Through this

Purpose Will Prevail

process, God taught me how to trust Him for each one of my needs.

I got on my knees and said, "Okay, God. I trust you as my provider. I need you now." God met every one of our needs on a day-to-day basis. He gave us exactly what we needed on that day, and we were never without. Was it hard? Yes, but I keep declaring and speaking the Word of God. I was declaring what God spoke to my spirit instead of what I saw. I became very familiar with the Word, which caused me to put it to action. I had to talk to myself daily. It went a little something like this: "Jasma, be not dismayed; Jasma, in all circumstances, be content and give praise; Jasma, give thanks, no matter the situation." This was my routine, and after I declared my daily declarations for the day, I was able to walk through my day with confidence. God was faithful and supplied all my needs. *And my God will meet all your needs according to the riches of his glory in Christ Jesus (Philippians 4:19, NIV).*

God was teaching me to trust him with everything—my purpose and my life. Even though the pressure was great, it changed me for the better. For instance, I have a greater compassion for people and what they go through. If somebody is hurting, my heart breaks because I know what it is like to hurt and have nothing. How can I speak to hurting people if I have never hurt? How can I speak to somebody about faith if I have never had to believe God for something? How can I help someone get delivered if I have never been delivered before? God has a purpose and reason for everything and already knows the beginning from end, which is why we have to trust God with everything. Whatever God says He is going to do, believe Him because He cannot lie.

If you think your purpose is too big to do it alone, then great! You are in a perfect place to trust the creator. If there is no trust, there is nothing. God likes when situations are impossible because they can only be made possible through Him. *For with God nothing will be impossible (Luke 1:37, NKJV).* We have been on a journey, one I believe that has changed your life and has activated your ultimate purpose. It is now time for you to stop living your surface-level life and be released into a deeper level of living. Are you ready?

Being confident of this very thing, that He who has begun a good work in you will complete it until the day of Jesus Christ (Philippians 1:6, NKJV).

Purpose Will Prevail

⋯ Prayer ⋯

Father, in the name of Jesus we thank you for divine knowledge and understanding. Father, thank you for allowing us to trust you completely with our lives and purpose. Father, blow our minds by completing a great work in us. Father, let your divine will be done in our lives. Father, no matter the circumstance or situation, we trust you. Father, thank you for taking us to a new level of trust in you.

In Jesus Name,
Amen

REFLECTIONS

Purpose Will Prevail

REFLECTIONS

10

Divine Release into Purpose

For it is God who works in you to will and to act in order to fulfill his good purpose

(Philippians 2:13, NIV)

It is time for a divine release into your ultimate purpose. The time is now, so be careful not to sit around and play with what God has placed inside you. You have all the tools, strategies, and keys to walk in your purpose with no fear and to fulfill it completely. As I speak of the divine release into purpose, I am reminded of the calling of the first disciples. Let's take a look at Matthew 4:18-22, *Walking along the beach of Lake Galilee, Jesus saw two brothers: Simon (later called Peter) and Andrew. They were fishing, throwing their nets into the lake. It was their regular work. Jesus said to them, "Come with me. I'll make a new kind of fisherman out of you. I'll show you how to catch men and women instead of perch and bass." They didn't ask questions, but simply dropped their nets and followed.*

A short distance down the beach they came upon another pair of brothers, James and John, Zebedee's sons. These two were sitting in a boat with their father, Zebedee, mending

Purpose Will Prevail

their fishnets. Jesus made the same offer to them, and they were just as quick to follow, abandoning boat and father (Matthew 4:18-22, The Message).

As we read this story of Jesus calling the first disciples, we see that they were doing their regular work in their career field; they were fisherman. They were living just a surface-level life, but were in preparation for purpose. Although the job you work is not your purpose, it still teaches you important discipline and principles. When it was time to walk in purpose, they dropped everything and followed Jesus. This amazes me because this story tells of the kind of presence Jesus walked with. The Bible states that they didn't ask any questions, but simply dropped their nets and followed Jesus. They came upon two others to whom Jesus spoke with the same authority, and they were just as quick to follow, abandoning the boat and their father.

Are you willing to drop everything and follow Jesus? Are you willing to leave your daily routine to answer the call and walk in purpose? We have been doing other things for so long, rejecting the yearning to do more in our spirits. I don't know about you, but I want to sense that feeling the disciples felt when Jesus called them. Their lives completely changed within a blink of an eye. Are you willing to get out of the boat and abandon any and everything to fulfill your purpose? Take a deep breath, step one foot out of the boat, take another deep breath, say Jesus I trust you, step out with the other foot, and then say God use me.

Don't get back into the boat. Instead, walk in your purpose with confidence and authority, remembering that you have everything you need to fulfill your purpose. Don't go back to old thinking and living. Don't revert because of the discomfort and pressure. Keep pushing because you will soon birth something great. I don't care what you have been through, what label people put on you, or what sin you have committed, God has a purpose for your life. I am messed up, and I need Jesus in my life. Every day I am becoming more and more like Jesus. You know my story, but no matter what I went through, it never stopped me from walking in my purpose. I pushed, and now I am birthing what God has placed inside of me.

I had a recent experience that changed my life. I wanted to go to a conference in Ohio, and so I asked a friend to go with me. We went to the conference, and we experienced God in a new and different way. We tasted of the Lord, and He was surely good. There was a well-known prophet at the conference who was calling people by first and last name. The presence of God was so heavy that you knew He was in the room. I had been through so much over the years and longed for an authentic touch from God. I heard God say, "I am about to call your name," and I was thinking to myself, *Yeah, right. This is me talking.* I kid you not, maybe three minutes later, this man called me out by my first and last name, and God spoke some awesome things to me. I was in awe the whole night. It took a while for my spirit to calm down. It wasn't the word that captivated me; it was the fact that God called me by my name. This man didn't know me, I didn't know him, but we knew the same God.

Purpose Will Prevail

This experience was a divine appointment for me. God was saying that now is the time. I am calling you to walk in your purpose now. Your way is done. It is my way now. Since that moment, I have never been the same. I have not been able to look at God the same. He is so real to me, and has proven Himself to be mighty on my behalf many times. I knew that I had been called years ago to fulfill a plan God had laid out for me, but I let life and distractions get in the way of my purpose. Don't miss your divine opportunity with God. Answer the call.

We live in a time where things are getting worse and the sight of things in the natural are getting bad, but don't be dismayed. God is still in control and has a plan. No matter what happens in your life, no matter what distractions come your way, no matter the opposition you face, I am here to tell you *purpose will prevail*. As you go through the process of purpose, understand that it all happens for a reason and God has a plan. Your calling has been activated in your life; you have been divinely released to walk in your ultimate purpose.

Important keys to remember:

- You were designed with a purpose.
- Sin separates us from God and the purpose we were created for.
- Purpose was restored and activated when Jesus died on the cross.

- The process of purpose is needed to effectively walk in your purpose.

- Break any addiction, habit, or sin that tries to hinder your walk with God and abort your purpose.

- Break the spirit of fear that keeps you from fulfilling your purpose.

- Accepting fear opens the door for other spirits to come in.

- Protect your purpose with everything in you.

- Speak life to your purpose and watch it unfold.

- Trust God with your purpose regardless of the circumstances.

- Accept the call and purpose God has for your life; you will not regret it.

- *Purpose will prevail!*

We humans keep brainstorming options and plans, but GOD's purpose prevails (Proverbs 19:21, The message).

Only God can tell you what your purpose is. My goal is to get you to a place in your spirit where enough is enough, and you become ready and willing to walk in your purpose. Don't ignore the passion and the drive you have in your spirit; this is for a reason. This is the passion that keeps speaking to your heart. This is the passion that will

Purpose Will Prevail

help you change the world and turn it upside down for God's glory. If you have a crazy dream that lines up with the Word of God, it's surely a part of your purpose because it will require His help. Finding your purpose is only doing what comes naturally when you are walking with God.

We also have to understand the importance of timing. Seasons are important in the kingdom of God. We are always in a certain season in our lives that is needed for what we are called to do. You will never just sit and wait around for anything to fall in your lap; it always takes active participation to see dreams and purposes fulfilled. We are always in preparation and training to be fully equipped and effective in what we are called to do. *To everything there is a season, A time for every purpose under heaven* (Ecclesiastes 3:1, NKJV).

Your calling is to serve people, but we were all created for different reasons to serve people. Everything in this world is evolved around people. Your purpose in serving people is unique because you have something that only you can offer. There is only a certain amount of people that I will be able to influence, but you, my friend, were born to influence the rest. The result in you fulfilling your purpose glorifies God, our Father, because you are fulfilling what He created you to do. I don't know about you, but all I want to hear Him say is well done, my good and faithful servant. *His lord said unto him, well done, thou good and faithful servant: thou hast been faithful over a few things; I will make the ruler over many things: enter thou into the joy of thy lord* (Matthew 25:21, NKJV).

When walking in your assignment, there will be moments of testing, but it's okay. The call is worth every test. Everything you do affects your purpose, so be careful to make every decision with God's guidance. I have failed many tests and have tried to go my own way, but I kept hitting a brick wall. I was trying to make opportunities happen when it wasn't time. We have to wait and let God exalt us in due season. Trust me, you will know and there will be no doubt in your heart that you are walking out your assignment because God will literally blow your mind.

You may have great things happening in your life, but is it your calling? When you walk in purpose, doors open that no man can close. What's yours is yours! Being divinely released into purpose is an amazing feeling because *you know that you know* that you were chosen to release your unique assignment into the world. You are released to be you, the authentic you, not the representative that wants everybody to like you.

Opportunities and divine connections will find you. Your blessings will chase after you. When I say God will meet your needs, He will do just that. He will impart divine wisdom, knowledge, revelation and the creativity for you to get it done. There is this sense of joy and completeness because the void has been filled. Embrace your journey. Most of all, walk with God through your journey. It's marvelous!

However, as it is written: What no eye has seen, what no ear has heard, and what no human mind has conceived the

Purpose Will Prevail

things God has prepared for those who love him (1 Corinthians 2:9, NIV).

... *Prayer* ...

Father, in the name of Jesus, thank you for clarity on purpose and the urgency to know what the call on our life is. The urgency to know our purpose and fulfill it. Father, thank you for tools, strategies and principles on how to walk out our purpose according to your will. No matter the circumstance or situation, you have given us supernatural strength for the journey. Father, thank you for peace that surpasses all understanding. Thank you for the divine release into a season of purpose and of greater. Father, let your will be done!

In Jesus Name,
Amen

REFLECTIONS

REFLECTIONS

BIBLIOGRAPHY

Daniels, K. (2013). *The Demon Dictionary.* Lake Mary, Flordia : Charisma House.

Directors, A. B. (2011, April 19). *American Society of Addiction Medicine.* Retrieved Decemeber 6, 2014, from American Society of Addiction Medicine: http://www.asam.org

fear. (n.d.). Collins English Dictionary - Complete & Unabridged 10th Edition. Retrieved February 05, 2015, from Dictionary.com website: http://dictionary.reference.com

land of nod. (n.d.). *The American Heritage® New Dictionary of Cultural Literacy, Third Edition.* Retrieved February 05, 2015, from Dictionary.com website: http://dictionary.reference.com/browse/land of nod

Mellman, T. A., Aigbogun, N., Graves, R. E., Lawson, W. B., & Alim, T. N. (2008). Sleep paralysis and trauma, psychiatric symptoms and disorders in an adult African American population attending primary medical care. *Depression & Anxiety (*1091-4269), 25(5), 435-440.

persona. (n.d.). *Online Etymology Dictionary.* Retrieved February 05, 2015, from Dictionary.com website: http://dictionary.reference.com/browse/persona

Rachel Gurevich, S. P. (2013). *Birth Plan for Dummies.* Hoboken, NJ: John Wiley & Sons, Inc.

Purpose Will Prevail

Ronald F. YoungBlood, F. B. (2004). *Nelson's Compact Bible Dictionary*. Nashville, TN: Thomas Nelson.

ABOUT THE AUTHOR

Born and raised in the small town of Robbins, Illinois, **Jasma Starks** later moved to Omaha, Nebraska to obtain her BA in Psychology and a Master of Arts in Human Service. She also has certificates in professional life coaching. Her educational background and strong passion for empowering people to accomplish their personal and professional goals in life has led to her success as a life coach, entrepreneur, and empowerment speaker.

A powerful prayer warrior, Jasma has the remarkable ability to make God's word plain and understandable. With a heart to spread the gospel throughout the world and elevate the name of Jesus Christ, she has devoted her life to teaching this generation of believers how to hear the voice of God and align their ways with His in order to take their lives from mediocre to extraordinary.

Currently residing in St. Louis, Missouri, Jasma seeks, wholeheartedly, to please God in all her ways while

Purpose Will Prevail

implementing progressive change in her circle of influence. In March of 2015, she birthed *Purpose will Prevail* to activate passionate people to walk in their divine purpose.

For more information, be sure to visit
www.JasmaStarks.com

How has this book transformed your life?

Jasma would love to hear from you!

TALK ABOUT IT ON

 JasmaStarks MsJasma

www.ingramcontent.com/pod-product-compliance
Lightning Source LLC
Chambersburg PA
CBHW052050070526
44584CB00017B/2114